PUTTING THE TRINITY BACK IN THE CHURCH

Putting the Trinity Back in the Church

Karl E. Shadley

RSM PUBLISHING HOUSE
BERKELEY, CALIFORNIA

© 2008 Karl E. Shadley
All rights reserved

RSM Publishing House
1460 Kains Ave. Berkeley, California 94709
www.revshad.org

Printed by
Lulu
www.lulu.com

Printed in the United States of America

Library of Congress Cataloging-in-Publication Data

Shadley, Karl E., 1952-
Putting the trinity back in the church /
Karl E. Shadley

Unless otherwise noted, Bible quotations in this publication are taken from the New Revised Standard Version Bible, copyright © 1989, by the Division of Christian Education of the National Council of Churches of Christ in the United States of America.

For Myrna

*my companion on
this wonderful journey of faith*

Contents

Acknowledgements		xi
Preface		xiii
Part I	**Our Relationship with God**	21
Chapter 1	The Trinity and Worship	23
Chapter 2	The Biblical Witness	33
Chapter 3	The Birth of the Doctrine	47
Chapter 4	Theological Development	57
Part II	**The Church's Worship**	81
Chapter 5	The Shape of Worship	89
Chapter 6	The Practice of Worship	113

Part III The Church's Mission		129
Chapter 7	The Shape of Mission	131
Chapter 8	The Practice of Mission	149
Part IV Preparing the Church for the Trinity		157
Chapter 9	The Pastor	159
Chapter 10	The People	169
Conclusion		175
Postlude		179
Biography		181

Acknowledgements

I am indebted to many people in the preparation of this book.

I am grateful for the generosity of the members of Village Presbyterian Church and Calvary Presbyterian Church for places to practice (and I mean practice) ministry but also for the gift of sabbatical time for reflection and writing. All my church communities have been very generous places for my practice of ministry.

I am thankful for my friend Margaret Kolberg who in her careful attention to detail spent untold hours collecting quotes, proofing, and filling in the spaces that supported my work all the while giving me the encouragement to finish the work.

I will always be indebted to Fuller Theological Seminary and the Doctorate of Ministry Program that required this dissertation and gave me the opportunity to study under some amazing teachers.

I am grateful for the people who have supported me in the formation process. The names are too numerous to print here but those who standout for me today are; Walter Ray who first introduced me to the idea of a practical Christian Community, Jack Loo and the many hours in a coffee shop helping me understand the place where my ministry fits in the big picture of convent theology, Harry Dorman whose patient listening to the details of my life helped me understand how God is God of even the little things of my life, Eugene Peterson with whom I had the opportunity to study under for two weeks and whose books gave voice and support for an authentic ministry and James Torrance who first baptized my imagination with the vision of a lively, Trinitarian, Incarnational understanding of God in my life and world.

Lastly I thank my family for all their support and inspiration in writing this book over the years. It is in relationship with my family that I truly understand what it means to live in community.

Preface

We have many rituals in worship. Each Sunday morning a particular ritual was played out with one of the youngest members of a small congregation. The liturgy was based on goodness. If the child was 'good' in worship, she was retrieved by the handsome young pastor to join him greeting at the door. I have been told that it was quite a reward for this young girl. But the liturgy was not without its drawbacks. If by chance, she squirmed or wiggled and upset the mood of the day, the result was to be passed over, left in the lurch. "Shame on you," was the silent congregational response. Not hard for a five year old to imagine the pointing finger of God leading the response. It still stings some sixty years later.

    I would like to think this is an uncommon experience in the church, but it is not. Like the lessons this child learned each Sunday, we too find ourselves approaching God, not as our benevolent benefactor who is always seeking ways to redeem us and bring us home; on the contrary, the God we approach all too often is a judging vindictive God looking for us to 'squirm' or 'wiggle', take a step off track, say a harsh word, think a wrong thought, and duck before lighting strikes.

    The burden that most people live with is how they can please a holy God. They try to do it on their own and when that fails they are told to turn to Jesus.

Putting the Trinity Back in the Church

Jesus is loving and kind. Jesus stopped to help strangers, hung out with thieves. Jesus understands. He has known temptation; He knows what it is like to lose your temper; He has felt the inner struggle, the battle of flesh; He has known the urge to give up, call it quits. If not for Jesus, who would understand and love us on Sunday morning?[1]

Professor James Torrance says that our theology too often makes the God of the Old Testament the harsh bad guy who then requires us to know a compassionate and loving Jesus to protect us from God's judgment.[2] It is my regular experience in counseling to hear people speak of how they believe they will get into heaven because of what they have done or have not done to please God. Often just the fact they have not been as bad as someone else is the 'grace' that would seem to be their salvation. It often sounds like little more than wishful thinking that maybe, just maybe, they will somehow slip by.

When it comes to the Holy Spirit, the mainline church has done a superb job of partitioning off the work of this dimension of the Trinity from the everyday life of the Church. We have relegated spirit talk to Pentecost Sunday or allowed it to be taken over wholly by those who speak in tongues or

---

[1] Evelyn Underhill understands this problem with people in the worshiping community when she makes this observation about worship, "In practice, of course, the equality of this triune revelation of reality is seldom observed. For many Christians, devotion to our Lord's Person is the sum of worship." Evelyn Underhill, Worship (New York: Crossroad, 1936), 64.

[2] James Torrance is a retired professor and head of the Department of Systematic Theology at the University of Aberdeen in Scotland. Though he is not the only scholar to see the importance of bringing the doctrine of the Trinity into the active life of the church, he is one of its greatest spokespersons. James can bring the Trinitarian Incarnational dogma alive as he lives out his convictions in his life and ministry. His success in presenting this model for ministry and worship has brought about reconciliation in the lives of people as far a field as Ireland and South Africa. I am indebted to James Torrance for the seed from which this dissertation has grown.

Preface

participate in fantastic forms of healing.

It is to this sad state of popular Christian practice and belief (theology) to which I address this book.

The Christian life should not be about finding our own resources to be presentable to God or hiding behind Jesus (who then turns out to be less than God). The life of the Church should not have to remove itself from the work of the Holy Spirit because it has been taken over by the "Charismatics" and "Pentecostals." The life of all Christians should be about living joy-filled, God-filled lives, lived in the full knowledge of God's abundant and life-giving love revealed to us in Jesus Christ and empowered by the Holy Spirit.

This is a message addressed to both church members and the pastors who lead them. "We cannot be throwing people back on themselves; that gives them nothing."[3] (as people like the Apostle Paul, Luther, and Calvin found out long ago).

We need to invite people into a relationship with God that does not depend on their goodness. We need to present to people a gospel message that does not put Jesus in the role of our protector from a harsh and demanding God of judgment. The good news is not that Christ comes to protect us from God, but that in Christ the true nature of God is revealed and shared with humankind. And not only is God's nature revealed in Christ but by the power of the Holy Spirit, we are invited to share in the very nature of God. Torrance calls it "the gift of participation" as we come to be part of God's Trinitarian/relational nature.

The good news of the gospel is that in Jesus Christ we are called into community with God, not on our merits, but on Christ's merits, and not by our devices but in and through the unmerited love of God, revealed in history through the life and ministry, death, and resurrection of Jesus Christ. We know of this wonderful gift not only from history but through the life of the Spirit of God at work in us and for us and through us and with us. I believe it is only when we encounter God in the

---

[3] This is a quote from class notes taken at Professor James Torrance's class on "The Ministry of Worship" in the Doctor of Ministry program at Fuller Theology Seminary, June 3-14, 1991.

fullness of God's revelation to us as Father, Son, and Spirit that we know the breadth of what God has done and can do for us. Anything less than an encounter with the full revelation of God, as Father, Son, and Spirit, leaves us encountering a God other than the one we meet as "Good News" in Holy Scripture. My purpose in writing this book is two-fold. First, to present a model of ministry that centers on a Trinitarian Incarnational[4] model of worship, and, secondly, to build a case for the belief that in initiating and leading worship with this emphasis, the pastor fulfills the most important role of the ministry to which she or he is called.

It is my premise that if pastors do a good job of leading the church in worship and if the worship they lead reflects a Trinitarian Incarnational view of the nature of God, then they are serving the church in the most effective way possible. Every other act of ministry grows rightfully out of the work of leading the congregation in worship. It is in worship that we find our understanding of grace, receive joy, experience community, are healed and heal, and find the motivation and the shape of our Christian Service. It is through worship that the pastor can lead the people toward a passionate, growing, effective Christian life.

One of the concerns that lead me to write this book is that worship is often not at the center of that which shapes the present nature of the church. Even when we do come to worship, our worship experience is often only a reflection of our ideas and inventions using the means that have proven "effective" and "successful." The means, then, of leading worship are largely evaluated by their ability to entertain as we seek to draw people to our community, (be it the X-Generation, Baby Boomers, Buster etc.).

The truth is that no matter how arousing our worship

---

[4] I use the term 'Trinitarian Incarnational' in my speaking about the doctrine of the Trinity to clarify my particular understanding of the doctrine of the Trinity. The doctrine of the Trinity is often limited to explaining the closed, inward relationships of the Godhead. A Trinitarian Incarnational view of the doctrine sees God's relational nature as outward and inviting to all creation. (I have borrowed this term from James Torrance.)

Preface

might be, it is not truly Christian worship unless its primary purpose is to call us into a reality of worship that is led by Christ and empowered by the Holy Spirit. A Christian community that measures the quality of worship by its own expertise in presentation runs the great risk of missing out on the essential experience of entering into "the worship of heaven" in which only Christ can lead us.

If we do not find the definition for what the shape and nature of the Church is to be in worship, we are in grave danger of losing our identity as the Church of Jesus Christ altogether. J.J. von Allmen sees worship as the only way the church can find its true nature, "...by its worship the Church becomes itself, becomes conscious of itself, and confesses itself as a distinctive entity. Worship thus allows the Church to emerge in its true nature."[5]

I have another concern as the church has lost its understanding of the central and distinctive role that worship plays in the life of the church. The pastor has acquiesced to the pressures of trying to serve the church as therapist, business manager, social activist, small group expert, church growth consultant, etc. In the process, the pastor has lost her/his principal role as worship leader in guiding and nurturing the people of the church.[6]

It is a fairly recent development in church history to stress the program of the Church over the worship of the Church in the transforming of the lives of its members. Since Old Testament times, congregational worship has been the means of bringing people into a relationship with God that has the power to transform lives. The early Church's success in transforming its world was achieved by bringing people near to God as they enter into Christian Worship. It was through its

---

[5] J.J. von Allmen, Worship: its Theology and Practice (New York: Oxford University Press, 1965), 42.

[6] I would not limit worship to Sunday morning. The pastor calls people to worship in many settings but the goal is always the same, to lead people into the worship that is led by Christ and calls people to enter into the worship that God has initiated.

worship that Christians experienced the story of salvation as their story and encountered the person of Christ in the Sacraments. The Reformation was fueled by a renewed emphasis on entering into the life of Christ through the worshiping community, in their culture, and in the home.

Today, seminary preparation very often stresses a different agenda for the work of the pastor in leading the church. Would-be pastors are steeped in specialized ministries such as small group development, church growth principles, counseling technique, and community organization as the basic means of transforming the lives of their people. Worship is more valued as a place of celebrating success and dazzling entertainment than as the primary place of meeting God and growing into the image of Christ. Eugene Peterson (Presbyterian pastor to pastors and author) has observed this problem in the American pastorate,

> The pastors of America have metamorphosed into a company of shopkeepers, and the shops they keep are churches. They are preoccupied with shopkeeper's concerns--how to keep the customers happy, how to lure customers away from competitors down the street, how to package the goods so that the customers will lay out more money.[7]

The shopkeeper model of ministry, which Peterson describes, has a particularly damaging effect on all pastors but can be particularly frustrating for pastors of smaller churches. While the pastors of larger, multiple staff churches are able to "do" all the things that are expected of a "shopkeeper," the smaller church pastor faces an insurmountable task in trying to perform tasks that were never, and should never be, part of the call to pastoral ministry.

Though the damage this modern model of Christian ministry does is more pronounced in the lives of small church

---

[7] Eugene H. Peterson, Working the Angles (Grand Rapids, Michigan: Williams B. Eerdmans Publishing Company, 1987), 1.

Preface

pastors, I believe it takes its toll on all pastors who have been led away from the classical roles of ministry to which Christian pastors are called. In an attempt to meet this marketplace agenda, the pastor moves away from the primary task of her/his ministry and is set up for frustration and, eventually, failure.

It is my assertion that pastors can best serve their congregations by making worship the guiding and primary focus of their ministry. This worship focus for ministry must be embraced by pastors if they are to lead their churches in appropriate and faithful ways.

I will develop this book in four parts.

In the first part of this book, I will present a Trinitarian Incarnational model for understanding our relationship with God. I will show that this Trinitarian Incarnational model of life with God is what shaped the early churches' understanding of the nature of worship. I will also examine the changes made in worship by the reformers of the sixteenth Century and how this Trinitarian Incarnational model influenced these changes. In this section I will also look at some recent attempts to redefine theological models of the doctrine of the Trinity.

The second part of the book will look at the ways that a Trinitarian Incarnational doctrine of the Trinity shapes the nature of worship in the church. I will also examine how this kind of worship can be practiced in the church.

In the third part of the book I will examine how this Trinitarian Incarnational model of worship affects and shapes the mission of the Church and how this particular approach to theology informs our lives in many other ways.

The fourth part of the book will look at ways to prepare the Church for a Trinitarian Incarnational model of worship and ministry. I will take a new look at the nature of pastoral ministry and examine how this insight affects the lives of church members. It is my goal, in this book, to give back to pastors a call to ministry where the central focus is the initiation and leading of Trinitarian Incarnational worship. This should not take away from the present mission that the church engages in nor should it negate the introduction of new creative means of serving God's people. This centering on worship would only serve as a focus for the whole ministry of the church. I believe if pastors comprehend and embrace the power of Trinitarian Incarnational worship to transform the lives of their people, it will give new health, vitality, and direction to their ministries.

PART I

OUR RELATIONSHIP WITH GOD

To start with worship as the Church's center is to start all our conversations in the context of a preeminent relationship with our God. This conversation is mediated by the work of Christ and the indwelling of the Spirit. To center our life together, in the context of worship, is to say that our conversation with God must come first in order to understand everything else about our lives. It is only when we can see our relationships, our work, our families, our very existence in the light of who we are in God's eyes that we can understand what it is to be a child of God. It is in Christian worship that we can regularly experience a relationship with Father, Son, and Holy Spirit as we live in union with Jesus Christ.

J.B. Torrance is a wonderful advocate for the Trinitarian Incarnational quality of worship,

> Worship is...the gift of participating through the Spirit in the Son's communion with the Father-- of participating, in union with Christ, in what He has done once and for all on the cross, and in the presence of the Father and His mission to the

Putting the Trinity Back in the Church

world.¹

Though worship has always held an important place in the life of the church, I believe worship has been overlooked as the primary source of life for both the Church and the individual Christian on too many occasions. What the Church needs is an understanding of worship that is flush with Trinitarian content. What the Church needs is a worship experience that can bring all God's people to the place where they can experience God's promise of Christ in them and they in Christ.

---

[1] J.B. Torrance, "Worship and the Gospel of Grace" (Unpublished paper for class," Ministry of Worship"), 3.

CHAPTER 1

THE TRINITY AND WORSHIP

In recent years we have come to look for new ways to draw people to the Church. Churches have sought to be more appealing to people by selling worship in terms that they hope will relate to our contemporary society.[1] My fear is that worship has been misused as a tool for evangelism and a form of "entertainment this morning."[2] It seems instead of classic

---

[1] J.J. von Allmen, Worship, 53. von Allmen takes aim at these abuses of Christian Worship when he writes "Worship as a means of 'character building' and of producing 'socially motivated personality' worship as a means to 'self-fulfillment' and 'success,' invitations to worship in the vein of 'come to church this week, you'll feel better, do better, live better, it's the American Way'--such are the more noxious expressions."

[2] Hughes Oliphant Old, Guides to the Reformed Tradition: Worship (Atlanta: John Knox Press, 1984), 3. "If today American Protestant worship services have confused worship with art, or even worse, if we have confused it with entertainment, it is because we have failed to fathom the meaning of the second commandment."

Putting the Trinity Back in the Church

Christian Worship holding the central place honor in the life of the Church, it has been altered by what are seen as more pragmatic approaches to designing worship.[3] It is not unusual to find a pastor leaving seminary well trained in the disciplines of family therapy, sociology, and church growth while receiving little training in the disciplines of worship and liturgy. This leads to the possible, and often realized, mistake of making worship the poor-step-sister when it comes to bringing people into a personal relationship with God.

One of the goals of the Reformation was to restore Sunday worship to its central and rightful place,

> It was hoped that Sunday--the day of the Resurrection, the feast of the Incarnation, the celebration of the Atonement--would be seen as the goal and the source of all other congregational activities.[4]

We would do well to have the same goal for our churches today.

There are many who perceive worship to be the primary place of transformation and personal spiritual growth for Christians, but the temptation in my own tradition today is to replace worship as the center from which we work. The movement is to replace corporate worship with a more effectual and seemingly productive agenda. I feel it is important to

---

[3] Duane Arnold and C. George Fry make the observation that pragmatism is a dangerous guiding force in the worship of American Churches today. "It seems to us that pragmatism as an ethic of worship has indeed had a profound effect upon the church in America. We have become absorbed by the desire to measure and evaluate our worship services by criteria which have little to do with our calling as ministers of the Good News of Jesus Christ" Page 2 of an article in compuserve's "Worship Forum."

[4] Willimon, William H. and Robert L. Wilson, <u>Preaching and Worship in the Small Church</u> (Creative Leadership Series ed. by Lyle Schaller, Nashville: Abingdon Press, 1980), 39.

present a theology of worship that can bring us back to an understanding of the place of worship as the regular means available to the Church in the transformation of the world for God's glory.

TRINITARIAN WORSHIP

I believe it is only in worship which reflects the importance of God's triune presence with us that we can really bring people to a place where they can experience the transforming power of God in their lives.[5]

True Christian worship can only take place when we are led by the one who leads us in worship as the one "true worshipper," Jesus Christ. It is as we participate in the joyous fellowship of the Father and the Son, in the power of the Spirit, that we can come to know what it means to be Christ's Church and experience the gift of being the Children of God. This, and only this, kind of worship can give back to the church a worship experience that will serve to fulfill the glorious and powerful worship of heaven in its midst.[6]

The reason worship has lost this central place in the life of the Church is because we have allowed it to be watered down by forces that are contrary to its biblical and theological

---

[5] Old, Guides, 8. "Worship is the workshop where we are transformed into his image."

[6] It would not be hard to sell to most Christians the notion of coming to a worship service that promised the adventure and blessing described in the Revelation of St. John "And I heard a loud voice from the throne saying, 'See, the home of God is among mortals. He will dwell with them as their God; they will be his peoples, and God himself will be with them; he will wipe every tear from their eyes. Death will be no more; mourning and crying and pain will be no more, for the first things have passed away.' Then he said to me, 'It is done! I am the Alpha and the Omega, the beginning and the end. To the thirsty I will give water as a gift from the spring of the water of life. Those who conquer will inherit these things, and I will be their God and they will be my children.' Revelation 21:3-4,6-7.

underpinnings. As we have found ourselves seemingly losing ground in the race for influence in our world, we have given in to the temptation of the wisdom of this age. We have chosen to be utilitarian and pragmatic in our approach to shaping worship. We have had more faith in what is thought to work than in what is true.[7]

We have not been faithful to what is biblical and sound theologically in designing our worship practice. The end result is that worship, as we often experience it, no longer has the vitality that it once had to empower the church and create a new people in God.

The church can try so hard to engage people "where they are" that it can lose sight that the purpose of worship is first and foremost to engage God and enter into the life of our triune God. Worship, then, is not primarily a time of teaching or motivational speeches or topical addresses about how to raise your kids or the things to do to have a successful marriage. All that we do in worship needs to point to an encounter with God which proclaims the communal nature of God's relationship with God's people as attested to in the Churches' doctrine of the Trinity. Everything else that the church calls ministry grows out of this central act of the Christian Church.

We in the Church are not left to our own devises in how to encourage this encounter with God. In John Peterson's excellent study of the biblical text relating to worship, he comes to the conclusion that God not only initiates worship but God also gives us directives of *how* to worship. To some extent the practices of worship are in fact a revelation from God. Christian Worship must heed divine revelation in its formulation of

---

[7] There is a video being marketed that is intended to help other churches follow the model of one very successful church in presenting the gospel message in contemporary ways. The content of the video is a series of "skits" dealing with contemporary problems which are to be used in worship. The use of these skits could most definitely lead to a pragmatic shaped service. It is not that you can't do a skit in worship and still be acting out Trinitarian worship, but the temptation is great to make worship a place to meet people's perceived needs instead of meeting the Triune God.

The Trinity and Worship

worship. Though there is a great deal of latitude in designing worship in different times and places, there is still a nucleus of revealed insight that must guide the content of the worship service.

I see the lack of a clear Trinitarian understanding of the nature of God as an inhibitor to full and effective worship in the Christian Church. James Torrance believes that the Church today professes a Trinitarian faith but in practice it is unitarian. By unitarian I mean an understanding of worship that misses the full communal nature of God in revelation. This unitarian worship sees God as the one who forgives us, befriends us, and saves us, but it misses the dynamic of entering into the presence of God as revealed in God's Trinitarian nature. Unitarian worship depends on what we DO in worship. In this view of worship, the people of God are always at an arm's distance from God. God can be a comfort as Father; God can be a savior as Jesus; God can even be involved in our lives as Spirit, but if we do not know God as passionately inviting us into God's relational, triune nature, the truly good news of the Gospel is lost. It is not what we do, but what God does in us that transform us into the people of God's image and goodness. A Trinitarian understanding of worship brings the people of God "into" the worship of God. It is a model that embraces the early Churches' understanding of what was new and transforming in their relationship with the God of Creation.

This has been the crux of James Torrance's message as he seeks to present to the Church a doctrine of the Trinity that enlivens the Church and its people. He believes that it is the doctrine of the Trinity that allows us to understand the truth about redemption which is revealed in Scripture and embraced by the early Church and the reformers.

In her book, God For Us, Catherine Mowry LaCugna makes this bold statement: "Christianity and Christian theology simply cannot do without a Trinitarian doctrine of God that articulates the heart of this faith."[8] It is my conviction that this assertion is also true of Christian worship.

---

[8] Catherine Mowry LaCugna, God For Us: The Trinity and Christian Life (San Francisco: Harper, 1973), ix.

Putting the Trinity Back in the Church

In part one of this book I will present the biblical, historical, and theological foundations for worship that are based on a Trinitarian Incarnational view of worship. I believe that when we make sure that a Trinitarian Incarnational model of worship is the defining principle in the life of the church, then we are less likely to fall prey to the tendency of adding extra frills to worship in order to add life to the service. Trinitarian Incarnational worship guides us in entering into the wonderfully full worship that grows out of our communion with God through the mediation of Christ in the power of the Spirit.

Ray Anderson understands how this approach can be a corrective in shaping ministry. "This Christological, and actually Trinitarian, basis for ministry rules out both utilitarianism, which tends to create ministry out of needs, and pragmatism, which transforms ministry into marketing strategy."[9] I believe we can build this Trinitarian basis for ministry through a life of worship that reflects such a Trinitarian understanding of our life with and in God.

The heart of the Christian message is not that we have a God whose great delight is to condemn creation for its sinfulness. On the contrary, the good news is we know a God who has revealed herself fully in the life, death and resurrection of Jesus Christ and by the power of the Holy Spirit has crossed the gulf which has separated us from God and brought us back into God's household. It is this desire for relationship with all creation which has been at the heart of God's will for us for all time.

This understanding of worship grows out of a new look at the way we view the doctrine of the Trinity. Though most theologians accept the idea of the Trinity as orthodox, it does not seem to have much, if any, effect in the practice of the Church.

Catherine LaCugna has done a great service to the church in taking a new look at the doctrine of the Trinity in her book <u>God for Us</u>. Her insightful observation has been that the doctrine of the Trinity as understood in the church today is "...a

---

[9] Ray Anderson, ed., <u>Theological Foundations for Ministry</u> (Edinburgh: T. & T. Clark, Ltd., 1979), 8-9.

The Trinity and Worship

doctrine of the Trinity that most consent to in theory but have little need for in the practice of Christian faith."[10] We will look more at LaCugna's work in chapter three of this book. Many other contemporary theologians who have an interest in the doctrine of the Trinity see this same neglect of this important doctrine.[11]

A major focus of this work will be building a foundation for a theology of worship which places the doctrine of the Trinity in the central role of defining what Christian Worship is for the church. This foundation will be built on the corner stone of biblical revelation.

My first exposure to the doctrine of the Trinity came in the form of physical, tangible models intended to illustrate "the nature" of the Trinity. These models were well intentioned but ultimately lethal explanations of the Trinitarian nature of God.

The most intriguing model for me was that of water, ice, and steam, one substance expressed in three different ways. Though the idea was interesting, in the end the model lacked the ability to express anything near the heart of the message of the Gospel. Though the doctrine of the Trinity originally grew out of the early churches' need to explain the mystery of how God could be present to us as Father, Son, and Holy Spirit and still be one God, these popular models only look at the philosophical question of how three things can be one.

It is a shame that for most of Western Christendom these inadequate models are as far as we ever get in our investigation and experience of the Trinity.[12]

---

[10] LaCugna, God For Us, ix.

[11] Ted Peters analyzes many contemporary approaches to the doctrine of the Trinity in his book, God as Trinity: Relationality and Temporality in Divine Life (Louisville, Kentucky: Westminster/John Knox Press, 1993).

[12] A member of the church I serve shared another possible model for understanding the Trinity. She discussed the image of my being Karl, a father, and a son, and that I was still one, like God in the Trinity. Again a good image, but when I asked her what difference it made, she really couldn't answer. The reality is that all the images of God locked up in

Putting the Trinity Back in the Church

Dorothy Sayers takes up the question of how the average churchgoer understands the doctrine of the Trinity when she puts these words in their mouths: "The Father incomprehensible, the Son incomprehensible, and the whole thi incomprehensible. Something put in by theologians to make it more difficult-- nothing to do with daily life or ethics."[13]

This is a typical problem with an understanding of the doctrine of the Trinity in the church today. The doctrine of the Trinity is seen as beyond the regular church members' understanding. The Trinity is seen either as a mystery beyond our human minds to understand (so why bother?) or as a "tacked on" doctrine that only confuses the matter of our understanding of God. This is not just the case with "regular church members" but also with many theologians. Cyril Richardson, in his book on the Trinity, states that the doctrine of the Trinity is crippled by "inherent confusions" because it is an "artificial construct."[14] I do not believe that the doctrine of the Trinity is an artificial construct but rather central to the early teaching of the church and the revelation of God.

The problem that often exists today in our understanding of the doctrine of the Trinity is that somewhere along the way this portrait of the nature of God was distorted from its original intent. A doctrine that once touched at the very heart of what it means to be in relationship with the Creator in intimate and passionate ways became a mystery beyond our understanding, or at best a mathematical formula attempting to unlock the mystery of God's objective person on high.[15]

God's self (inter-relationship) do not touch on the redeeming truth of the Gospel and so are of little interest (as it should be) to us.

[13] Dorothy Sayers, <u>Creed of Chaos</u> (New York: Harcourt, Brace and Co., 1949), 22.

[14] Cyril Richardson, <u>The Doctrine of the Trinity</u> (New York: Abingdon, 1958), 53.

[15] Anthony Kelly, <u>The Trinity of Love</u> (Wilmington, Delaware: Michael Glazier, 1989). In this book Kelly takes a refreshing look at the doctrine of the trinity in light of the work of Barth, Rahner and those

The Trinity and Worship

The Right Question

There are a number of historical reasons for this trend. The basic problem in understanding the meaning of the Trinity is that we have been asking the wrong question of the doctrine. The question that the doctrine of the Trinity speaks to is not *what* God is (all wrapped up in God's self) but on the contrary, *who* God is and *how* God then acts. As John Leith says "The unity of God is personal, not mathe-matical"[16]...but mathematical it has become. So the questions we ask of the doctrine of God's unity must be personal *who* questions if we are to understand the power of the Trinity as it affected the first generation church and its people, and so an investigation into what God has done and is doing.

In the process of trying to answer the *what* question about God, the doctrine of the Trinity lost its meaning for practical Christian living and particularly its meaning in relationship to worship. Catherine LaCugna is not surprised at this development seen in the context of her study of the history of the Trinity;

> Because of the particular direction the history of dogma took, many people now understand the doctrine of the Trinity to be the esoteric exposition of God's 'inner' life, that is, the self-relatedness of Father, Son and Spirit (sometimes called the 'immanent' Trinity). But if this doctrine

---

who have followed in their steps. Kelly makes this delightful comment about the selling out of the Trinity "I have always felt that something was deeply wrong when it (the doctrine of the Trinity) has usually been regarded not only as ineffable but unspeakably, well,...boring, if that is not too strong a word. Certainly, it has caused something of a mental block to both student and teacher and preacher (the dreaded Trinity Sunday homily!)." This is a very good book working out of a renewed interest in an alive doctrine of the trinity for the church community today.

[16] John H. Leith, <u>Basic Christian Doctrine</u> (Louisville, Kentucky: Westminster/John Knox Press, 1993), 49.

can speak only of a Trinity locked up in itself and unrelated to us, then no wonder so many find it intrinsically uninteresting.[17]

SUMMARY

This was not the way an idea of the Trinitarian nature of God was embraced by the early church. Before a formal doctrine of the Trinity was established in the fourth century the idea of an inner-relatedness of God in Father, Son, and Spirit was an active, relational concept that was paramount to the understanding of how God relates to God's people; that is, how it is found in the liturgy of the early church.

The doctrine of the Trinity does not have to be cold or irrelevant. The doctrine of the Trinity points to a much greater truth as it presents to us a dynamic understanding of how we can be caught up in the story of salvation as revealed in the story of scripture.

---

[17] LaCugna, God For Us, 2.

CHAPTER 2

THE BIBLICAL WITNESS

The scriptural witness reveals how First Century Christians understood the way the God of creation chose to be involved in the lives of Christians through the work of Christ and the Spirit.

Any Christian Doctrine of God's Trinitarian nature must be created and formed by our understanding and exposure to the scriptural witness. It is God's redemptive acts in history that the doctrine of the Trinity is trying to explain, nothing more, nothing less. For the doctrine to be a true and faithful servant of God's revelation to us, it must always be tested and find its only substance in the powerful words and work of God.

In our study of Scripture, we will see how the Christians of the first century understood the redemptive work of God as Father, Son, and Holy Spirit.

In the letter to the Hebrews, we will investigate how the early church understood the work of God in Christ in light of the Old Testament practice of worship and will pursue the implications of that model for Christians in the writings of 1 Peter.

In a study of Paul's writings, we will gain insight into how the early church embraced the possibility of finding unity with God through the work of Christ and the intervention of the Holy Spirit.

The Letter to the Hebrews

One of the jobs of the Church in every generation is to find ways to explain their faith in terms that are intelligible to the world and yet remain faithful to the Gospel as they know it (and as it was passed on). This was a particularly difficult job for the early Church. Their task was to create a doctrine of faith that could explain all that they knew to be true about their experience and knowledge of Christ. Some of their sources for doctrine came from the teaching of Israel, though everything they borrowed from Israel's creed was now to be seen through the experience of Christian faith. Some of their language was developed by the early apologist using common experience and knowledge to explain the uncommon event of God with us.

The end result of their activity was a doctrine of faith that was firmly established in the witness of salvation history revealed in Israel and Christ but also grounded in the language and experience of their contemporary setting. It is to this early witness of the doctrine of the Trinity that we now turn.

One of the ways the writer of the Letter to the Hebrew's describes the work of Christ is as a fulfillment of the role of High Priest. Using the Old Testament role of High Priest as an archetype, the writer describes how it is that Christ is able to bring them into a right relationship with God.

The writer of Hebrews describes the role of the priest as one of intercessor between the people and God. Ideally, the High Priest, acting for himself and in behalf of the people, was to make blood sacrifices for the atonement of their sins. The end result of the work of the high priest was to make it possible, through sacrifice and inter-cession, for the people to come into the presence of God and be reunited with their creator.

The writer's thesis is that with the coming of Christ, the old ways of the Temple are revealed as ineffective and temporal; "Thus it was necessary for the sketches of the heavenly things to be purified with these rites, but the heavenly things themselves need better sacrifices than these"(Hebrews 9:23 NRSV). In Christ they now have a true High Priest, whose work of redemption is effective and eternal; "he entered once for all into

The Biblical Witness

the Holy Place, not with the blood of goats and calves, but with his own blood, thus obtaining eternal redemption" (Hebrews 9:12 NRSV). No longer does the day of atonement need to be repeated yearly to make up for its temporal nature, but now our atonement has been secured once-and-for-all in the sacrificial death and resurrection of Jesus Christ; "We have this hope, a sure and steadfast anchor of the soul, a hope that enters the inner shrine behind the curtain, where Jesus, a forerunner on our behalf, has entered, having become a high priest forever according to the order of Melchizedek" (Hebrews 6:19-20 NRSV).

In the letter to the Hebrews, we see how the early church understood that the work of Christ was God working in their behalf to secure their redemption and so restore their relationship with God. What had been revealed to the Israelites in signs was made real for Christians by the work of Christ in human history. "They offer worship in a sanctuary that is a sketch and shadow of the heavenly one..."(Hebrews 8:5 NRSV).

For the writer of Hebrews, Jesus Christ is not a priest who is detached from the people. On the contrary, Jesus Christ is very active in the lives of the people for whom he mediates; "Consequently he is able for all time to save those who approach God through him, since he always lives to make [intercession] for them"(Hebrews 7:25 NRSV) and He understands them, "For we do not have a high priest who is unable to sympathize with our weaknesses, but we have one who in every respect has been tested as we are, yet without sin"(Hebrews 4:15 NRSV).

The reality for the writer of Hebrews is that Jesus Christ has taken on human nature; "Therefore he had to become like his brothers and sisters in every respect, so that he might be a merciful and faithful high priest in the service of God, to make a sacrifice of atonement for the sins of the people" (Hebrews 2:17; see also Hebrews 2:11 and 3:14 NRSV).

One of the most profound insights of this writer is that Jesus not only represents the people before God in his own person, but he invites the sinner to enter into the salvation he has already made ready for them. "...but we do see Jesus, who for a little while was made lower than the angels, now crowned with glory and honor because of the suffering of death, so that by the grace of God he might taste death for everyone"

(Hebrews 2:9 NRSV). P.T. Forsyth expresses wonderfully this belief of participation in Christ; "Christianity is not the sacrifice we make, but the sacrifice we trust; not the victory we win, but the victory we inherit."[1]

The writer of Hebrews also sees the universal and timeless nature of Christ's ministry when he asserts, "Consequently he is able for all time to save those who approach God through him, since he always lives to make intercession for them" (Hebrews 7:25 NRSV).

The writer of Hebrews shows his debt to the practices and convictions of Israel in understanding his own convictions. It is through the sacrificial practices of Israel that the writer can make sense of Christ's redeeming sacrifice on the cross. It is through the priesthood of ancient Israel that he is able to understand Christ as the High Priest who can in fact secure His redemption.

James Torrance sums up the teaching of Hebrews in this way: "When Christ assumed our humanity, for our sakes consecrated Himself, in our name suffered, died, rose again, ascended to the Father, we suffered, died, rose again, and ascended to the Father in Him. We entered into the presence of God in the Person of our High Priest."[2]

The writer of Hebrews reveals an understanding of who God is and how God works that can later be spoken of in terms that are consistent with the later churches' doctrine of the Trinity. Though the writer of Hebrews does not use the word Trinity, it is important to note that the theological material of Hebrews would never support a view of the Trinity that sees God locked up in God's self.

The theological material of Hebrews can only be

---

[1] Donald G. Bloesch, The Future of Evangelical Christianity (Colorado Springs: Helmer and Howard, 1988), 8. Though this is a quote from P.T. Forsyth, Bloesch did not have a reference to the Forsyth's work.

[2] J.B. Torrance, "The Place of Jesus Christ in Worship," in Theological Foundations for Ministry Ray S. Anderson, ed. (Eerdmans Publishing, Grand Rapids, Michigan, 1979) 353-4.

The Biblical Witness

contained in a Trinitarian view that has God seeking to reach out, even at great personal cost, to be involved in the lives of God's people. A doctrine of the Trinity that is only interested in God's inner life is not faithful to the scriptural witness of the Letter to the Hebrews. Only a doctrine of the Trinity that reveals God's nature as relational and inviting to all creation can hope to shed any light on the true transforming nature of God.

First Peter

The writer of 1 Peter extends this Old Testament model for the work of Christ into our lives when he makes the connection between the work of Christ and the work that we are called to do. When he states "But you are a chosen race, a royal priesthood, a holy nation, God's own people, in order that you may proclaim the mighty acts of him who called you out of darkness into his marvelous light,"(1 Peter 2:9 NRSV) he is not declaring that the Old Testament idea of priest should be re-established in the Church. With Christ as our true High Priest, we have been invited to share in Christ's ministry by God's grace.

It is seen in the Letter to the Hebrews that the early biblical writers embraced the belief that the sacrificial life and death of Christ was more than a model for life or an act that stirs our compassion. As God works out His plan of salvation in history on the cross, Christ has become the guarantor and source of our salvation. It is not what we accomplish but what He already accomplished for us that was Good News to the new Church.

Paul's Letters

Though the concept of living in union with Christ is present in the letter to the Hebrews, this doctrine of being in 'union with Christ' is more fully developed in the letters attributed to Paul.[3] Let us look at Paul to understand the way

---

[3] "Paul, whose message is our primary source for the doctrine of union with Christ..." Lewis B. Smedes, Union with Christ, A biblical view of the new life in Jesus Christ (Grand Rapids, Michigan: William B. Eerdmans Publishing Company, 1970), xi.

the early church and its 'theologians' perceived what God was doing in the work of Christ.

The ability to live *in union with Christ* represented the most radically new understanding about how God enters into history and into the lives of His people. The letters of Paul are replete with the image of our lives being lived in union with God. Paul makes use of many different images in describing the Christian living her/his life in union with Christ.

We are seen as participating in and becoming the body of Christ. We now have the heart and mind of Christ. We experience death without Christ, but are now found alive in Christ. We are brought into the Family of God as joint heirs and brothers and sisters with Christ, and are now the beloved children of God and are given the voice to cry Abba, Daddy, with Him. We who were strangers and aliens are now brought into the citizenship of the Kingdom of God. It is the old self that has been crucified with Christ, and we have put on a new self, becoming a new creation, and have received a new humanity in Christ. We have been clothed with Christ and are growing up into Christ in maturity and stature. We are told that Christ now dwells in us, and we are seen as a building that has Christ as its cornerstone. We are like plants, rooted and grounded in Christ and becoming conformed to the Image of Christ.

The sheer number of images and references to living in union with Christ alone shows the importance of this tenet in the belief system of Paul. A reading of Paul's writings reveals over one hundred references to the union of believers with and in Christ through the many metaphors used by Paul.[4]

When Paul boldly declares "I have been crucified with Christ; and it is no longer I who live, but it is Christ who lives in me..." (Galatians 2:20 NRSV), he is not jumping to conclusions. This declaration comes at the end of a long theological journey full of personal struggle as well as great joy. Though he uses metaphors to describe what has happened to us in Christ, this

---

[4] Though the images of "in Christ," "with Christ," and "Christ in us" can be seen as different aspects of the doctrine of union with Christ, I will deal with all three collectively under the heading of union with Christ. For a detailed study of these three different aspects of Paul's thought on unity, see Lewis B. Smedes, Union with Christ.

The Biblical Witness

central event he describes is very real to him. In his communication with the Church, Paul seeks to find new terminology to share this totally new and unheard of event.

The most important part of being in union with Christ is that our union with Christ is a means of being in a personal and healing relationship with the God of Creation. Just as the writer of Hebrews saw Christ as the High Priest in whom we have access to God, Paul saw that it was in Christ that a sinful people could find the grace to enter into the joy of God's presence in their lives.

Paul sees God's desire to be intimate with his people as deeply seeded in His nature. "...as God said, 'I will live in them and walk among them, and I will be their God, and they shall be my people...and I will be your Father, and you shall be my sons and daughters, says the Lord Almighty,'"(2 Corinthians 6:16,18 NRSV). Paul understood that this Old Testament promise and aspiration of God had now come to fruition as revealed in the ministry of God through Christ and the Spirit.[5]

We see in Paul an understanding that at the heart of God's desire was God's plan of salvation. "...he has made known to us the mystery of his will, according to his good pleasure that he set forth in Christ, as a plan for the fullness of time, to gather up all things in him, things in heaven and things on earth" (Ephesians 1:9-10 NRSV). "For we are what he has made us, created in Christ Jesus for good works, which God prepared beforehand to be our way of life" (Ephesians 2:10 NRSV).[6]

Again Paul uses a number of images to encompass the

---

[5] Here are just a few of the passages that refer to the pledge made by God and revealed in the Old Testament writings, "At that time, says the LORD, I will be the God of all the families of Israel, and they shall be my people" (Jeremiah 31:1 NRSV). "My dwelling place shall be with them; and I will be their God, and they shall be my people" (Ezekiel 37:27 NRSV). "...and I will bring them to live in Jerusalem. They shall be my people and I will be their God, in faithfulness and in righteousness" (Zechariah 8:8 NRSV).

[6] Also see Galatians 4:4-7 NRSV

idea of this new found relationship with God. We are the body brought together by God through Christ. We are a heavenly family, members of the household of God, and sons and daughters of God chosen for adoption by His good pleasure and will. We are to see ourselves as a holy temple in the Lord, citizens with the saints. We are told that we once were far from God but now we are brought near. Paul can only do justice to our new relationship with God in terms and images of family warmth and security.[7]

For Paul, our God is not an indifferent observer, but He moves in to feel our sorrow, to know our joy, and to share our loss. God, in Christ, has come to live not just with us, but, by the power of the Spirit, He now lives "in us!" He is not a God who is removed in any way, but "He has become what we are that we might become what He is."[8] Calvin has called it the "wonderful exchange," Christ's life for ours!

It is Paul, in his conversation with the fledgling Church, who gives the people of God a doctrine that can fully embrace the reality of their experience. It is in union with Christ that they find redemption and the way back into loving communion with God. "Therefore, since we are justified by faith, we have peace with God through our Lord Jesus Christ, through whom we have obtained access to this grace in which we stand; and we boast in our hope of sharing the glory of God"(Romans 5:1-2 NRSV).

The early church embraced the teaching of Paul as they experienced the reality of what Paul and others taught. It was Paul's onslaught of image after image, coming from every angle, cradled in the context of everyday language and experience that was able to do justice to the wonderful truth of the Gospel. The Good News was in need of a language to contain it and a voice

---

[7] The many references to adoption are particular touching to my family as we are in the long process of adopting our five year old foster son.

[8] I first heard this quote in James Torrance's class "The Ministry of Worship," at Fuller Theological Seminary, in June of 1991. I have now traced this quote to Irenaeus.

The Biblical Witness

to proclaim it, and the Church found that voice in the language of relationship.

It was in a very real and loving relationship with Christ that the early church could discover the nature of God's love for them. The words of union with Christ were central in their understanding of the work of God in Christ. It was this doctrine that became their primary means of understanding what God was doing in the Church and in their lives. I think that Lewis Smedes speaks for the early Church when he says, "He touches us here and now, not merely by the ripples of the historical currents He once set in motion, but by entering into union with us personally."[9]

This realness of union with Christ was not just thought of as spiritual but was a union that was physical; "For while we live, we are always being given up to death for Jesus' sake, so that the life of Jesus may be made visible in our mortal flesh"(2 Corinthians 4:11 NRSV).

The Holy Spirit and the Trinity

To understand the full nature of the doctrine of the Trinity, as it was being developed in the early church, it is helpful to take a special look at the role the Spirit played in the early church's understanding of its new-found relationship with God.

To deal with the role of the Spirit in a separate section seems necessary to counter the trend in recent times to either over play the role of the Spirit in the Church (as in the charismatic movement) or to nearly ignore the role of the Spirit altogether (as in most all other churches). An active and meaningful doctrine of the Trinity can be a corrective that places the role of the Spirit in its proper and biblical perspective.

It seems that for the first Christians it was the work of the Spirit that gave power and presence to the idea of God with us in Christ. Calvin saw the importance of the Spirit in uniting Christ with His people,

Christ is "present to those who believe in Him in

---

[9] Smedes, Union with Christ, xi.

the greater energy of the Spirit; He lives in them and dwells in their midst and even within them." The Spirit, as Calvin often says, is the mysterious bond between the Lord 'out there' and His earthbound disciples. The Spirit is the power of Christ to overcome the 'ugly ditch' between Him and us.[10]

If we visit again the passages that inform us about the Christian's unity with Christ, we see that the work of the Spirit is vital to understanding the complexity of this reality.

It is the Spirit which gives us life in Christ and dwells in us, "But if Christ is in you, though the body is dead because of sin, the Spirit is life because of righteousness. If the Spirit of him who raised Jesus from the dead dwells in you, he who raised Christ from the dead will give life to your mortal bodies also through his Spirit that dwells in you" (Romans 8:10-11 NRSV).

It is the Spirit which helps us in our weakness and teaches us to pray, "Likewise the Spirit helps us in our weakness; for we do not know how to pray as we ought, but that very Spirit intercedes with sighs too deep for words. And God, who searches the heart, knows what is the mind of the Spirit, because the Spirit intercedes for the saints according to the will of God". (Romans 8:26-27 NRSV).

It is the Spirit by which we are adopted as children and can join with Christ in calling God Abba "For all who are led by the Spirit of God are children of God. For you did not receive a spirit of slavery to fall back into fear, but you have received a spirit of adoption. When we cry, "Abba! Father!" it is that very Spirit bearing witness with our spirit that we are children of God," (Romans 8:14-16 also see Gal.4:6-7 NRSV).

It is the Spirit that guides us "If we live by the Spirit, let us also be guided by the Spirit" (Galatians 5:25 NRSV) and gives power "I pray that, according to the riches of his glory, he may grant that you may be strengthened in your inner being with power through his Spirit" (Ephesians 3:16 NRSV).

The Spirit is a spirit of unity "making every effort to

---

[10] Ibid. 126.

The Biblical Witness

maintain the unity of the Spirit in the bond of peace" (Ephesians 4:3 NRSV).

It is by the Spirit we have access to the Father "for through him both of us have access in one Spirit to the Father" (Ephesians 2:18 NRSV) and through the Spirit that God's love dwells in us "because God's love has been poured into our hearts through the Holy Spirit that has been given to us" (Romans 5:5 NRSV).

We are told that the Spirit is given by God; "Now we have received not the spirit of the world, but the Spirit that is from God" (1 Corinthians 2:12 NRSV) and in fact the Spirit is God's Spirit: "Do you not know that you are God's temple and that God's Spirit dwells in you?" (1 Corinthians 3:16 NRSV).

Though this is not an exhaustive treatment of pneumatology in Scripture, it does show the importance of the Spirit in understanding the nature of God's work with and in Christians. It is through the work of the Spirit that allowed the church not to just ponder and admire the ideal of a Triune God but allowed them to experience the reality of the Trinity in their lives. It is by the real presence of the Holy Spirit, given to believers that Christians can enter into the life of God's Trinitarian nature.

The reality is that the work of Father, Christ and Spirit are so interrelated it is hard to identify who is at work at any one time. Lewis Smedes in his study of these passages concludes:

> (1) There is no clear distinction between Christ dwelling in Christians and the Spirit dwelling in them. (2) There is no hint that Paul is using metaphor, as though he really means only that an impersonal power is at work on us to make us somewhat Christ-like or Spirit-like. (3) It is clear that the Christ who is in us is the person named Jesus, the concrete individual who died and rose again. (4) The presence of Christ and the Spirit within Christians is not limited either to a few Christians or to odd moments. The presence of

Putting the Trinity Back in the Church

Christ within is normal for all Christians.[11]

Summary

There are still many other passages of Scriptures which would add to our discussion and give more detail to what we have already reviewed. For instance, a study of the final discourse of Jesus in the Gospel of John (chapter 17) could add more scriptural support for a biblical basis for an understanding of the Trinity. We could also look at Genesis 18 when the three men come to Abraham and Sarah. This passage has inspired many to better understand the ancient nature of revelation about the mystery of the Triune nature of the God of Israel.

We will stop here because no matter how much we look, we will not find a stated formal doctrine of the Trinity in the biblical text. A formal doctrine of the Trinity is a creation of the Church. It is not verbalized in Scripture; rather, it is a systematic attempt at explaining that which is revealed in scripture. Karl Barth writes in his Dogmatics that though the doctrine of the Trinity is not necessarily biblical, it does have its roots in the revelation of scripture.[12]

---

[11] Lewis, Union with Christ, 113.

[12] "This doctrine as such does not stand in the text of the Old and New Testament witness to God's revelation. It did not arise out of the historical situations to which these texts belong. It is the exegesis of this text in the speech, and this also means in light of the questions of a later situation. It belongs to the Church." Karl Barth, Church Dogmatics: Vol.1, Part 1, The Doctrine of the Word of God, ed. G.W.

The Biblical Witness

I believe that the doctrine of the Trinity, if understood in terms of a saving Trinity, is very much at the heart of the early church's theological understanding of what was being revealed to them through the biblical witness and the spirit. The development of a doctrine of the Trinity was a natural result of the churches' understanding of salvation history and quickly became part of its proclamation and worship (liturgy).

Bromiley, T.F. Torrance, Trans. G.W. Bromiley,(Edinburgh: T.&T. Clark, 1936, 1975), 375.

CHAPTER 3

THE BIRTH OF THE DOCTRINE

Though the early church had no formal doctrine of the Trinity, we can see from scripture they did think in Trinitarian terms of Father, Son, and Spirit. The understanding of the inter-relatedness of Father, Son, and Spirit was at the very heart of their understanding of the nature of God, but God's relational nature was not limited to the Godhead in relation with itself. A clear reading of Scripture shows that God's bold move to relate *to* and be *with* God's created ones in Christ, through the Spirit, was at the core of their testimony. There is no way to explain the life, growth, and power of the Church in the first century without this important understanding of the inter-relatedness of God.

History of the Doctrine

Though there was an understandable lack of a systematic doctrine of the Trinity in the New Testament writings, we can see a practical interpretation of the nature of God's being espoused in the very earliest writings of the New Testament. There has been a great deal of systematizing, analyzing, and categorizing of the contents, of these New Testament writings in the past two centuries but that is not to say that all this ensuing work has been an improvement on the original.[1]

What can surely be said about any study of the Trinity is that it must be faithful to what Paul, the writer of Hebrews, and other biblical writers have written. Just as these writers had to seek out an understanding of Christ in the light of the biblical canon of Israel, so theologians in any age now must 'do' their theology in the context of the Christian biblical canon. This to me would be the basic requirement of calling a theology "Christian."

The approach of this early theological work was very practical. From their writings, we can see that they were not interested in developing an esoteric doctrine of God. Everything they wrote and said (and we can be sure they said much more than they wrote) was aimed at sharing the incredible story of Christ and the way he could changes lives. The writers were more observers than they were philosophers. Their new doctrines of God were based on their understanding and experience of salvation history. Catherine LaCugna shows her indebtedness to the practice of these biblical masters in her method of study in considering God's character. "The mysteries of God's Covenant with Israel, of the cross and resurrection of Jesus, of new life in the Spirit, form the only solid basis for pondering the nature of God."[2] It is clear from our study of scripture that the overriding, driving theme of the early writers is that God is passionate about being in relationship with his people. Even though God has sought out a relationship with creation from 'the foundations of the world', a relationship with

---

[1] One such 'analyzer' has admitted to this very fact. In the last paragraph of Lewis Smedes 200 page book systematizing Paul's thought, he concedes, "I would like to add this only that there is also a defense for simply letting Paul's thought speak to us on its own....Perhaps we can assume that Paul provides us with a context that is in itself clear enough to tell us where the images fit in." Smedes, Union with Christ, 186-7.

[2] LaCugna, God For Us, 169.

The Birth of the Doctrine

God does not come without requirements for God's created ones. The relationship we have with God must be faithful, honest, open, and true. It must be a relationship that has integrity. The doors leading to this relationship are a clear conscience and a clean heart. It is seen from the testimony of the Old Testament that God will have nothing to do with a dishonest relationship.[3] The pressing question for people like Paul and other early Christian theologians was "What are the means to this right relationship with God for a helplessly sinful people?"

These early theologians could see that God dealt with this problem of human sinfulness through the giving of the Jewish cultic system, but the results were temporary and ineffective. Now 'in the fullness of time' God had come to make the situation right in Jesus Christ. It was in the light of the life of Christ that God's plan for history was made clear. It was this plan of God that was crucial to the belief of the early Church. It was the economy of salvation that was at the heart of the Christian message and was the content of the yet to be named and formulated, doctrine of the Trinity. LaCugna is very perceptive in summing up the relational character of the doctrine,

> The central theme of Trinitarian theology is the relationship between the pattern of salvation history (oikonomia) and the eternal being of God (theologia)...God by nature is self-expressive, God seeks to reveal and give Godself, God seeks to be united with other persons. This is consistent with the biblical images of a God who is alive, who is ineluctably oriented 'other-ward', who is plenitude of love, grace, and of mercy overflowing.[4]

---

[3] Psalm 1 compares those who are righteous and those who are wicked. Only the righteous can enter into presence of God. This is one of many passages that proclaim this truth about being in relationship with God.

[4] LaCugna, God For Us, 230.

It is LaCugna's assertion that these elements of the doctrine of the Trinity (what I would call a Trinitarian Incarnational doctrine and LaCugna calls an orthodox doctrine of the Trinity) are essential to a biblically faithful creed that can be practical for the life of the Church.

> In Jesus Christ, the ineffable and invisible God saves us from sin and death; by the power of the Holy Spirit, God continues to be altogether present to us, seeking everlasting communion with all creatures. Christianity and Christian theology simply cannot do without a Trinitarian doctrine of God that articulates the heart of this faith.[5]

This was the early shape of the doctrine of the Trinity, even if it was not yet named, which was embraced as essential to an understanding of the meaning of life in Christ.

In our study of worship it is interesting to note it was in the areas of the practice of religion that theology was, and still is, first developed. It was in worship that the doctrines were 'acted out,' then later systematized by the theologians.[6] It can also be said that it was in the liturgy that the doctrine of the Trinity was preserved when theology had created a doctrine with little meaning or interest for people of the Christian Faith.

The Fall of the Doctrine

If this Trinitarian Incarnational doctrine of the Trinity was so important to the early church why did it not continue to have the same impact on the church in later years?

As the doctrine of the Trinity was developed in the ensuing centuries, it lost much of its crucial, relational, features. In LaCugna's thoughtful study of the Trinity, she concludes that

---

[5] Ibid., ix.

[6] Legem credendi lex statuat supplicandi (The law of prayer founds the law of belief.) quote in LaCugna, God For Us, 112.

The Birth of the Doctrine

the doctrine of the Trinity lost its relational nature as it was developed in a theological battle to determine orthodoxy in the fourth century.

LaCugna believes that it was at the time of the writing of the Nicene Creed (fourth century) that the church separated soteriology and the doctrine of God. It was not until this time that the church sought to separate the inner workings of the divine life and the work of God in salvation history.[7]

The basic problem was that Arius and the Arians believed that the biblical accounts of the nature of Jesus relegated Jesus to the position of a lesser God because he was the one sent (begotten) by God. This stance was taken in trying to protect the monotheism faith of the Old Testament and in so doing protect the sovereignty of God, God transcendent. This assertion was so opposed to biblical revelation that there was a flurry of activity at this time to develop a systematic understanding of the relationship of what was to become the doctrine of the Trinity.

The response of those against Arius, and those who followed him, was to create a system that protected the equality of the revealed nature of God as Father, Son, and Holy Spirit. How this was accomplished was different in the Eastern (Greek) Church and the Western (Latin) Church.

The Latin Church found a basis for understanding the nature of the Trinity in Augustine. Augustine believed it possible to comprehend the Trinitarian nature of God by relating the image of God implanted in humans as the mirror of the divine image. In this way the church found its insights to God's nature by meditating on the image of God in us. With analogies like Lover-beloved-love, or memory-intellect-will, Augustine was able to perceive a doctrine of the Trinity that saw the three modes of God as different but equal. Augustine still saw God as first one but revealed to us as three coequal modes

---

[7] Though LaCugna thinks that J.N.D. Kelly, in his study of the Creeds, is right in believing that the Scriptural Witness required the early fathers to think in threefold terms of God, she thinks he goes too far in stating that the concept of the threefoldness of God was a part of Christian thinking from the start. LaCugna God For Us, 129.

sharing a common essence.

This understanding of the Trinity was effective in countering the thought that Jesus could be somehow lesser or subordinate to God but this line of thought also had its drawbacks when it came to describing the relational nature of God as revealed in scripture. By taking the course that God's Trinitarian nature is revealed to us by our own self examination of the imputed image of God in us, we miss the meaning of salvation history in defining God's nature. This formula of understanding the doctrine of the Trinity effectively locks God's relative nature in the realms of heaven and as God's heavenly nature revealed in us at our creation. LaCugna states the limits of Augustine's doctrine of the Trinity as "...the emphasis on interiority as the place to discover the Trinity has the effect of locating God's economy not in the history of salvation but within each human person."[8]

This understanding of the doctrine of the Trinity does not do justice to the biblical witness which presents God as not only relational in self but as outwardly relational to all creation.

The Greek Church took a different approach to countering the heresy of this time. The Cappadocians (Basil, Gregory of Nyssa, and Gregory of Nazianzus) sought to find equality in the Godhead by changing the understanding of the nature of origin. The Cappadocians asserted that Divinity originates with personhood, not with substance. As the Arians were trying to establish God's glory in God's autonomy as transcendent and self-sufficient, the Cappadocians alleged that God's revelation leads us to understand God from the point of personhood. This being true, then being-in-relation-to-another is the originating principle of reality. This being true, then LaCugna says that "If God were not personal, God would not exist at all."[9] This approach leads to an understanding of God as possessing extroverted love as God's very nature. This insight into the nature of God was not able to avert a movement in both

---

[8] LaCugna, Catherine Mowry, Ed. Freeing Theology: The essentials of theology in feminist perspective (San Francisco: Harper, 1993), 88.

[9] Ibid., 87.

The Birth of the Doctrine

the Western and Eastern traditions to see God's Trinitarian nature as a self-sufficient divine community.

Though a more elaborate development of how the fall of the Trinity came about is beyond the scope of this study, it is valid to say that from the fourth century on (though people like John Calvin were an exception) the inquiry into the nature of the Trinity has mostly been limited to the inward nature of God as revealed in the Godhead.[10]

LaCugna sadly defines the history of the doctrine of the Trinity as "the emergence and defeat of the doctrine of the Trinity."[11] The emergence of the doctrine is revealed in the writings of the New Testament and hinted at in the early development of the doctrine of the Trinity in the fourth century. At this stage the images and ideas behind the doctrine play a central role in integrating the many areas of doctrine developed in response to the revelation of Christ in history.

The defeat comes when the doctrine of the Trinity is limited to the study of God's nature in God's self. "The diversity and uniqueness of the divine persons within the economy of redemption faded into the background, and the centrality of Christology, soteriology, and pneumatology in the theology of God was diminished. Hence the defeat of the doctrine of the Trinity".[12]

---

[10] For a detailed history of this chapter in the history of the doctrine of the trinity refer to LaCugna's book God for Us, particularly refer to chapters 1 through 4. Also there is a good review of LaCugna's thoughts on the history of the doctrine of the trinity in Freeing Theology, 83-91.

[11] LaCugna, God For Us, 8.

[12] LaCugna builds her thesis on the foundation of "the emergence and defeat of the doctrine of the trinity according to the theoretical perspectives of both the Eastern and Western traditions (though to a lesser extent in the East), the divine persons eventually were relegated to an innerdivine realm locked up in itself, hidden from view, able to reach out toward the creature across a vast ontological chasm only though what the East came to call the mediation divine energies, and the West, a unsubstantial act." LaCugna, God For Us, 9.

Putting the Trinity Back in the Church

Limiting the doctrine of the Trinity to a study of the inner life of the Godhead has been very detrimental to the life of the Church. Instead of the knowledge of the Trinity opening us to an understanding of the relational nature of God in our world, the doctrine only becomes speculation into God's secret and hidden nature.[13] This speculation might be very interesting to philosophers but has shown to be of little interest to those embracing the faith as life changing.

The defeat of the doctrine of the Trinity was solidified during the period of The Enlightenment. A Trinity that was limited to God's inner nature "up there" was much more palatable to the enlightenment's reluctance to deal with the supernatural nature of the Christian Faith.

The harm caused to the church in losing a Trinitarian Incarnational doctrine of the Trinity was greater than we might realize. In losing an intra-relational model of God with God's people, the church lost a path of entering into a relationship with God that could lead to real transformation. The lack of a healthy and biblical doctrine of the Trinity also leads to the imbalance of emphasis between Father, Son, and Spirit in the life of the Church.

We can see from the methodology of the Biblical writers that images and ideas have the power to put people into places to understand the way God is working in our lives. Paul uses the everyday image of a body to try and touch on the relationships that we have with God and each other when we enter into life with Christ. The writer of Hebrews uses the Old Testament idea of high priest to point to the greater work of Christ that can bring human beings into the holy presence of God.

The images and ideas aren't redeeming in themselves, but they do point to a greater reality that allows people to

---

[13] "Eventually, however, the doctrine of the Trinity became concerned with only one side of this framework, namely, the intradivine relationality of God to God, thought of apart from the relationship of God to us through Jesus Christ and the Holy Spirit". LaCugna, <u>God For Us</u>, 12.

The Birth of the Doctrine

understand how God can work in their lives. Though the images are helpful, they only point to the work of God, in salvation, in much greater and more profound ways than the images and ideas could ever hint at.

The image and idea of the Trinity can be a doctrine that suggests the nature of our relationship with God. A doctrine of the Trinity that is faithful to the concepts emerging for the early biblical writers is a wonderful source of pictures and possibilities for the worshiping community. When the concept of the Trinity is seen as revealing the mystery of God's nature as relational and affable, it becomes a doctrine that has the potential to open the doors of our soul to the reality of "God with us." When the Trinity illustrates God's plan for creation as a passionate reaching out to redeem all that God has made, the worshipper is made ready for an experience of God's mercy and grace. When the idea of the Trinity is seen as a present reality, empowered by the activity of the Holy Spirit, the worshipping community is able to understand how it is that they can be made new in a world growing old. It is in this context of thought, that the Trinity is a reality of God's relationship with us, that we can not only celebrate God's work but actually participate in the divine work of salvation.[14]

A renewed doctrine of the Trinity speaks volumes to the nature of societal relationships as based on the image of God's nature that we in the church hold out as a model and inspiration.

When we come to worship believing that what God has done in the past is his will for our present and future, we come ready to become the Church of Jesus Christ in all its power and

---

[14] The use of icons has been particularly helpful in allowing Christians to understand the dynamics of the relational nature of the Trinity. LaCugna and Kelly relay in their writings the help that icons have played in their understanding and experience of the Trinity. Henri J.M. Nouwen offers a helpful guide to investigating the Trinity with the help of icons in his book Behold the Beauty of the Lord: Praying with Icons, (Indiana: Notre Dame, Ave Maria Press, 1987). My own meditation and visioning of the Trinity has been helped by spending time gazing on Andrew Rublev's icon depicting the Holy Family.

possibilities. It is this understanding of the Trinity that must be reclaimed by the Church in our day. LaCugna sees this as the direction that theology must take in order to be faithful to the biblical witness and meaningful to the Christian community. The only option for Christian theology is to be Trinitarian.

Summary

In embracing the doctrine of the Trinity as the source of revelation into the relational, passionate, outreaching, redeeming nature of God, I believe we will find ourselves enlightened and inspired by the same images and ideas that were at the heart of New Testament thought and inspiration. It is this symbol of Trinity that can assist the pastor in constructing "a world of meaning that orients human life toward God."[15]

I will now turn to the development of a doctrine of the Trinity that breathes new life into the life, worship and work of today's Church. The development of a Trinitarian Incarnational doctrine of the Trinity has great implications for the worship, and so the life, of our church today.

---

[15] Ted Peters builds on the use of symbols that were used in the Old and New Testaments to point to the reality of God's nature. He points out that God is not literally a king or a father or a lamb but that these symbols lie at the edge "where mundane reality intersects with the transcendent reality of God." Ted Peters, God - The world's Future: Systematic Theology for a Postmodern Era (Minneapolis: Fortress Press, 1992), 82-83.

CHAPTER 4

THEOLOGICAL DEVELOPMENT

As we investigate the development of the doctrine of the Trinity we will look at a number of theologians who have played a part in reviving interest in the Trinity.

I will start with Calvin and the Reformers. I will then look at the work of Karl Barth, Jurgen Moltmann, and Catherine LaCugna. I will end the chapter looking at the work of the British Council of Church's Study Commission on Trinitarian Doctrine Today.

Trinitarian Thought and the Reformation
We can best understand the tenets of the reformed faith in the light of an Incarnational/Trinitarian understanding of our worship life. It was this understanding of Christ as the true mediator of our worship that formed Calvin's understanding of grace by faith. It is not what we do that allows us to come into a restored relationship with God, but the work of Christ in us and for us that is our only hope for salvation. James Torrance reminds us of this in his reading of Calvin,

> "So Calvin expounded it at the time of the Reformation in the Institutes, Bk.II:Chaps.9-11ff; Bk.IV:Chaps.14-17 and also very fully in his

Putting the Trinity Back in the Church

Commentary on the Epistle to the Hebrews. This was the heart of his interpretation of baptism and the Eucharist, as of all worship, viz. that Christ's Baptism is our baptism, set forth in our water baptism; that Christ's Sacrifice is our sacrifice, set forth at the table; that Christ's Worship is our worship, set forth in our worship and prayers.[1]

Part of the work of reformers like Calvin and Luther was to create an evangelical worship that replaced the elaborate ritual system of the Later Middle Ages. At the heart of this transformation was an understanding of the abiding presence of God in the act of worship and experienced in the sacraments. This renewed understanding of God's presence in the act of worship opened the door for a new and life-giving relationship of the congregation with God.[2]

At the heart of the reformation was a new understanding of how people could be involved in a relationship with the God of creation. This is vividly seen in Calvin's understanding of the Lord's Supper.

Calvin had an insightful understanding of how Christ was present at the Eucharist meal. For Calvin, Christ's presence at the meal was not so much a local (physical) presence as a personal (spiritual though still very real) one. By the work of the Holy Spirit, Christ could be with us in the breaking of the bread but at the same time we could be with him in the banquet feast of the lamb. This understanding of Christ's presence was not temporal but seen as lasting. It was this personal union with

---

[1] J.B. Torrance, "The Place of Jesus Christ in Worship," in Theological Foundations for Ministry: Selected Readings for a Theology of the Church in Ministry Ray S. Anderson, ed. (Edinburgh: T & T Clark and Grand Rapids: Eerdmans, 1979), 350.

[2] In this section of her book, Underhill reviews the way that the reformers influenced the church of their day. Evelyn Underhill, Worship, (New York: Crossroad, 1936), 276-297.

Theological Development

Christ that was seen as the means to transformation into the image of Christ. The Eucharistic meal was a means for the faithful to enter into an intimate fellowship with God and by the blessing of this renewed relationship enter into a new kind of relationship with each other.

For Calvin, an open, relational Trinity was essential to his perception of the presence of Christ with his people. Calvin's understanding of the Trinitarian nature of God could not be caught up in a speculative understanding of the relational nature of God on high but was dependent on a doctrine of the Trinity in which the faithful could participate. His doctrine of the Trinity found its source in the biblical witness to a saving, redeeming, promise-keeping God.

> Calvin never ceased to be awed and amazed at the fact that in his familiar self-revelation as the Father, the Son and the Holy Spirit, God has given us access to knowledge of himself as he really is in himself, in the inner relations of his Triune Being.[3]

People who are influenced by Calvin's work would certainly be led to the importance of an Incarnational Trinitarian understanding of God in their worship and action.

Calvin's understanding of the nature of the Trinity and its place in the life of the church is one stepping stone that leads the church back to embracing the doctrine of the Trinity as essential to its work of understanding of the nature of God as relational. Calvin saw that any doctrine of God must rely on God's Trinitarian revelation in history, "...the only God we know is the God who has named himself to us as Father, Son and Holy Spirit. Apart from that Trinitarian knowledge of God, all we have in an empty idea of God fluttering in our brain."[4]

---

[3] Thomas F. Torrance, Trinitarian Perspectives: Toward Doctrinal Agreement (Edinburgh: T&T Clark, 1994), 76.

[4] This is a paraphrase found in from Thomas F. Torrance, Trinitarian Perspectives (Edinburgh: T&T Clark LTD), 75 of a quote in John Calvin, Institutes of the Christian Religion John T. NcNeill ed., Ford

A Renewed Interest in the Doctrine of the Trinity

The doctrine of the Trinity will always be an idea tucked away in the dusty corners of the philosopher's study until it is understood as a doctrine that has meaning in the life of the Christian person. A new interest in a Trinitarian God is being fanned by the works of a number of theologians. The root of this new approach to Trinitarian study is found in the work of Karl Barth who sets out a number of proposals which will guide others who follow him in their thinking about doctrine of the Trinity.

Karl Barth

Karl Barth, in the first volume of his Church Dogmatics, sets the stage for a new direction of study and renewed interest in the doctrine of the Trinity in modern times. The Editors of the English translation of Dogmatics say:

> In it (his works) Barth seeks to direct modern theology back to its patristic foundations in the dogma of the Holy Trinity, and to show that the root of the Church's understanding of the Trinity of God is to be found in God's revelation of Himself as the Lord.[5]

These same editors believe that Barth's work establishes the doctrine of the Trinity as the nucleus for all theological inquiry. "...The doctrine of the Trinity itself belongs to the very basis of the Christian faith and constitutes the fundamental grammar of dogmatic theology."[6]

Barth sees the doctrine of the Trinity as a reliable

Lewis Battles trans., (Philadelphia: The Westminster Press, 1960), 122.

[5] Karl Barth, <u>Church Dogmatics: Vol.1, Part 1, The Doctrine of the Word of God</u> G.W. Bromiley, T.F. Torrance, ed. G.W. Bromiley, trans. (Edinburgh: T.&T. Clark, 1936, 1975), viii.

[6] Ibid., ix.

Theological Development

testament of the Biblical witness to the revelation of God. He requires the church to build its doctrine of the Trinity on the solid ground of Scripture. He sees the doctrine of the Trinity as a logical and needed doctrine of the Church to address the pressing questions presented to it in the first centuries of its existence. Barth is very careful as he approaches the doctrine of the Trinity and its place in the study of God. He moves slowly as he sets the foundation for the place of the doctrine in the study of the nature of God. He is mindful of the mistakes that others have made before him.[7]

Though Barth recognizes that the doctrine of the Trinity is not found directly in scripture, he does see its roots in scripture,

> In calling revelation the root of the doctrine of the Trinity we are thus indicating that we do not confuse or equate the biblical witness to God in His revelation with the doctrine of the Trinity, but we do see an authentic and well-established connection between the two.[8]

He begins his analysis with a look at how we should approach the development of the doctrine of the Trinity. He does not want there to be any doubt that the doctrine is not formulated out of human experience. The only acceptable origin for the doctrine is from the revelation of God. Barth makes note that the doctrine is a formulation of the Church but only as it is inspired by the Biblical witness.

After establishing the Doctrine of the Trinity as an accurate representation of God's revelation of self, Barth goes on

---

[7] "Already in the early Church doctrine of the trinity was attacked on the ground that it is not biblical, that the form in which it was formulated by the Church's theology it cannot be read anywhere in the Bible...The Fathers of the Church and the councils, and much later the Reformers in their battle against the anti-Trinitarians, were naturally well aware that the doctrine of the trinity is not in the Bible." Ibid. 308.

[8] Ibid., 311.

to make the case that the doctrine is not only helpful in Christian Theology but that it is an essential doctrine.

> The doctrine of the Trinity is what basically distinguishes the Christian doctrine of God as Christian, and therefore what already distinguishes the Christian concept of revelation as Christian, in contrast to all the other possible doctrines of God or concepts of revelation.[9]

He would go as far as to say that doctrine of the Trinity is the essential doctrine for the Church in understanding the nature of God[10] and that denying the Trinitarian nature of God would lead us to be talking about a God other than the God of the Old and New Testament.[11]

Barth realizes in making the doctrine of the Trinity the starting point for the study of theology he is taking a different approach than most dogmatic theologians. "In putting doctrine of the Trinity at the head of all dogmatics we are adopting a very isolated position from the standpoint of dogmatic history."[12] Barth's point is that the very way we order our approach to the study of God shapes the conclusions to which we will eventually come. The Trinitarian approach to our investigation into the nature of God starts with discovering first WHO God is.[13] If we answer this question correctly, then we

---

[9] Ibid., 301.

[10] There is little doubt about the importance that the doctrine of the trinity holds for Barth when he states; "The doctrine of the Holy Trinity is the basic dogma of Christianity." Ibid., 302.

[11] "...in denying the threeness in the unity of God we should be referring at once to another God than the God revealed in Holy Scripture." Ibid., 360.

[12] Ibid., 300.

[13] "The first question that must be answered is; who is it that reveals Himself here? Who is God here? And then we must ask what He does and thirdly what he affects, accomplishes, creates and gives in His

Theological Development

can answer the question of what does God do and what does God effect?[14]

This is not a new idea for Barth but part of the influence of John Calvin on Barth's understanding of the doctrine of the Trinity.

> Hence Calvin rejected the theological method of the Latin schoolmen that began with the abstract question 'what is God' (quid sit Deus), and put in its place the concrete question 'what kind of God is he', (quallis sit Deus), which is a question about knowing what accords with the nature of God. That is to say, we may know God only in accordance with who he is (quis sit Deus) in his activity towards us and what he has revealed to us of his nature through Christ who as Mediator has come to reconcile us to himself.[15]

Barth is very clear as to the nature of God's unique revelation of God's self to humanity. He argues that the revelation that we experience of God in history is an accurate representation of who God is in God's self. God's revelation of self gives humanity a true picture of who God is and how God

---

revelation. But if the first question is intelligently put, when it is answered the second and third questions will be answered as well, and only when answers to the second and third questions are received is an answer to the first question really received." Ibid., .297.

[14] "In giving this doctrine a place of prominence our concern cannot be merely that it have this place externally but rather that its content be decisive and controlling for the whole of dogmatics. The problem of the Trinity has met us in the question put to the Bible about revelation. When we ask: Who is the self-revealing God? The Bible answers in such a way that we have to reflect on the Trinity of God. The two other questions: What does God do and what does He affect? Are also answered primarily, as we have seen, by new answers to the first question..." Ibid., 303.

[15] T.F. Torrance, Trinitarian, 41-2.

acts.

> If we really want to understand revelation in terms of its subject, i.e., God, then the first thing we have to realize is that this subject, God, the Revealer, is identical with His acts in revelation and also identical with its effects.[16]

Though Barth can say that God's revelation to us is indistinguishable from the very nature of what God is and does, Barth is also clear in explaining the limits of God's revelation.

Barth believes the scriptural witness is explicit in protecting God's sovereignty. Though all of God's acts of revelation are true and consistent with God's nature, God's revelation does not give humans any control over God. God is still free to act as God chooses in His autonomy. "God gives Himself entirely to man in His revelation, but not in such a way as to make Himself man's prisoner. He remains free in His working, in giving Himself."[17]

Barth is much more careful in protecting God's sovereign nature than many who follow him in proclaiming the virtues of the Trinitarian nature of God. Barth believes it is biblical and so critical to see God not only in the intimacy of his revealed self but also to recognize God's Holy otherness. The God who draws near to humanity in Christ is also the God who rules as Lord of all. Barth sees his warning as an echo of the biblical admonition,

> This reserve of Yahweh, His concealment even in His revelation, is also indicated by the urgent

---

[16] Barth goes on to say, "He(God) comes as the angel to Abraham, He speaks through Moses and the prophets, He is in Christ. Revelation in the Bible is not a minus; it is not another over against God; it is the same, the repetition of God. Revelation is indeed God's predicate, but in such a way that this predicate is in every way identical with God Himself." Ibid., 299.

[17] Ibid., 371.

Theological Development

warning in Ex. 3: 'Draw not nigh hither; put off thy shoes from off thy feet, for the place whereon thou standest is holy ground.'[18]

It is with these propositions of Karl Barth that most, if not all, other theologians start into the current conversation about the place of a doctrine of the Trinity in the church today.

Jurgen Moltmann

Though Jurgen Moltmann agrees with Barth that the place to start theological inquiry is with doctrine of the Trinity[19] they come at it from a very different perspective. Barth begins his inquiry from the perspective of God's unity that is revealed in the three persons of the Trinity. Moltmann sees the appropriate starting point of theological inquiry to be in the triune revelation of God.

The problem that Moltmann sees with Barth's approach is that by starting with God's unity he is stressing the sovereignty of God which leads to an inference of God's hierarchical domination over creation.[20] Moltmann sees this

---

[18] Ibid., 322.

[19] Douglas Meeks makes a bold statement in his review of Moltmann's major work on the Trinity, "Would anyone be willing to argue again that everything in the Christian faith is at stake in the doctrine of the Trinity? Yes, Jurgen Moltmann argues precisely this in the first volume of his `systematics',..." Douglas Meeks, 472.

As did Barth, Moltmann knows that he is taking a very different direction in theology when he uses doctrine of the Trinity as his theological hermeneutic.

[20] "...the germs are already present whenever idealistic modalism penetrates the Christian doctrine of the Trinity, threatening to disperse the three distinct persons and subjects the `history of the Son' in favour of `the One God'. Consequently we must be alive to these tendencies in even the best contemporary theologies." Jurgen Moltmann, The Trinity and the Kingdom: The Doctrine of God Margaret Kohl, Trans., (San Francisco: Harper & Row, Publishers, 1981), 140-1. Moltmann sees this as the very mistake that Barth made in his presentation of doctrine of the Trinity.

approach to the Trinitarian nature of God as Christian Monotheism. Moltmann sees this as limiting any real communication to a one way declaration from God to humans. Moltmann seeks to present a doctrine of God that respects an honest interaction of God with Humankind and all creation.

Moltmann sees the possibility for understanding a human relationship with God as a reciprocal relationship by starting with God's passionate expression of God-self in revelation.[21] Like Barth, Moltmann sees the need to begin his inquiry into the nature of doctrine of the Trinity from the biblical witness. His stress is on the narrative of the New Testament and the passionate God that we meet in the life of Christ.[22] The earthly life, suffering, death on a cross of Jesus is to humans a divine revelation to the nature of God. We do not have a God who is safely removed from human suffering, but in Christ we have a God who has known our grief and suffers with us. The cries of God's people do not go unheard and they are not inpassionately received.

Moltmann's approach to the doctrine of the Trinity does not start with God's unity that is then expressed in three modes but starts with the revealed nature of a Trinitarian God whose unity is found in the relationships. This has radical implications to our understanding of God as well as human anthropology and ultimately human society.

At the center of this discussion is the understanding of what constitutes freedom.

For Barth, God's freedom is found in God's ability to act as God chooses to act. In Barth's doctrine of the Trinity it was necessary to protect God's ability to act freely without any limits imposed by the intervention of human desires or needs. This was seen as the need to protect God's sovereign nature. Barth

---

[21] "if we are to understand the suffering of Christ as the suffering of the passionate God--it would seem more consistent if we ceased to make the axiom of God's apathy our starting point, and started instead from the axiom of God's passion." Ibid., 22.

[22] "The theology of divine passion is founded on the biblical tenet, 'God is love'(1 John 4:16)." Ibid., 57.

Theological Development

would say this grows out of the Biblical witness, though Moltmann would say it is influenced by an antiquated philosophical understanding of the nature of personhood.[23]

For Moltmann, God's freedom is found in God's ability to act out of God's very nature as a God of love. Moltmann sees true freedom the freedom to act not in any way one chooses but to act within a consistent pattern that reflects love at its deepest levels. God's having, by God's nature, to act in ways that are consistent with the loving, passionate God that we see revealed in the New Testament is not a limit to God's freedom but a true expression of freedom. That God does "react" to the cries and prayers of God's people is consistent with God's revealed nature. When God acts in such a way, God is only being who God is.

Moltmann points out that the problem with Barth's understanding of the nature of God's freedom is this understanding of divine freedom precludes human freedom.

> Which concept of freedom is appropriate to God? As we have seen, the nominalist concepts of freedom of choice and free power of disposal only have a very limited value for our understanding of God's freedom. They derive from the language of domination. In this language only the lord is free. The people he is master of are not free. They are his property, and he can do with them what he likes. In this language freedom means lordship, power and possession. It is this interpretation of freedom as power and lordship over possessions which is being theologically employed if we assume as our starting point that God reveals himself as 'God the lord'.[24]

---

[23] See Moltmann's discussion of this in The Trinity and the Kingdom, 139ff.

[24] Ibid., 56.

Putting the Trinity Back in the Church

This is unacceptable in Moltmann's understanding of God as revealed in the Jesus narratives of the New Testament. Moltmann supports his theses with writers from outside of the customary theological dialogue. One particularly intriguing insight into the passion of God, presented as the very nature of God, comes from G. A. Studdert Kennedy. Moltmann quotes from his book The Hardest Part.

> It's always the Cross in the end - God, not Almighty, but God the Father, with a Father's sorrow and a Father's weakness, which is the strength of love. God splendid, suffering, crucified - Christ. There's the Dawn. ... I want to win the world to the worship of the patient, suffering, Father God revealed in Jesus Christ...God, the Father God of Love, is everywhere in history, but nowhere is He Almighty. Ever and always we see him suffering, striving, crucified, but conquering. God is Love.[25]

For Moltmann a doctrine of the Trinity based on God's passionate revelation leads us to an understanding of the Trinity that is not only faithful to the biblical witness but leads to a new and just understanding of personhood and relationality in society.

Moltmann's doctrine of the Trinity is an understanding of God's nature not as patriarchal or as a monarchy. God is not God Almighty, rather God is humankind's loving friend. "...freedom does not mean lordship; it means friendship. This freedom consists of the mutual and common participation in life, and a communication in which there is neither lordship nor servitude."[26]

Moltmann calls his understanding of the doctrine of the Trinity an open Trinity. By this he sees a Trinitarian system that

---

[25] Ibid., 34-36.

[26] Ibid., 56.

Theological Development

invites humanity to participate in the divine Trinity.

> So the Trinity becomes an open mystery; its unity, the fruit of its communion, includes humanity and all creation; eschatologically, everything will be united in the Trinity...The history of salvation is the history of the eternally living, triune God who draws us into and includes us in his eternal triune life with all the fullness of its relationships."[27]

Moltmann's ultimate contribution to the Trinitarian dialog is the practical implication that a doctrine of the Trinity has for human relationships and society as a whole.

Moltmann believes that the old model of a closed Trinity with its patriarchal, almighty view of God is the model for an oppressive, inequitable society. He sees an open Trinity as the true model of right and just relationships between people. Jurgen Moltmann stresses that the community of the church and friends of Jesus should have the same relationship as the one revealed in the unique unity of the Father and Son.

> "Their community not only should reflect the community of the Father and the Son, but could also participate in the divine community of the Son and Father. This presupposes that the community of the Triune God is so wide open that as humanity and nature are united in love, the entire creation will find space and time in God. The unity of the Triune God is open and inviting for the unification of the entire creation not only with it but also in it."[28]

---

[27] Leonardo Boff, Trinity and Society, Paul Burns, trans., (New York: Orbis Books, 1988), 120.

[28] Elizabeth Moltmann-Wendel and Jurgen Moltmann, Humanity in God (Cleveland, Ohio: The Pilgrim Press, 1983), 88.

Putting the Trinity Back in the Church

The strength of Moltmann's work is the presentation of a doctrine of the Trinity that fits the New Testament witness of God's revealed nature in Jesus Christ. Our God is a passionate God who is not immune to our suffering. God's nature is to love without measure, never counting the cost of his love. God, because of who God is, can act in no other way.[29]

His work has very practical implications for worship as well. To understand the wonderful relationship between humans not as an unattainable dream but as a gift of a triune God to the people of faith opens new possibilities for the act of Christian worship. "History is swept into the divine life because the Trinity is an open Trinity."[30]

The weakness of Moltmann's work is his seeming obsession that his doctrine of the Trinity does not attach any connotations of hierarchy or sovereignty. Though he seeks to be guided by scripture in coming to his conclusions, his preoccupation with the liberation of humanity from any forms or models of unequal relationships seems to influence his results.

I don't believe we need to be exclusive in our understanding of God's nature as either an open Trinitarian or sovereign and above. A passage like Deuteronomy 4:29-33 reflects the nature of God as both sovereign over all as well as compassionate, open and involved in creation.

> From there you will seek the LORD your God, and you will find him if you search after him

---

[29] "Moltmann argues that if God is love, then God's freedom comes not in the freedom of either loving or not loving. God is bound to love. God is not compelled to love by outward necessity, but God evidently is compelled to express himself as he is and in no other way. Therefore, it follows that the triune God loves the world with the very same love that God in the Godself is." Ted Peters, <u>God as Trinity: Relationality and the Temporality in Divine Life</u> (Louisville, Kentucky: Westminster/John Knox Press, 1993), 106.

[30] Ibid., 103.

Theological Development

with all your heart and soul. In your distress, when all these things have happened to you in time to come, you will return to the LORD your God and heed him. Because the LORD your God is a merciful God, he will neither abandon you nor destroy you; he will not forget the covenant with your ancestors that he swore to them. For ask now about former ages, long before your own, ever since the day that God created human beings on the earth; ask from one end of heaven to the other: has anything as great as this ever happened or has its like ever been heard of? Has any people ever heard the voice of a god speaking out of a fire, as you have heard, and lived? (NRSV)

There is a new voice in the Trinity conversation who sheds light on a possible solution to the division between Barth and Moltmann or at least presents a new path for discovering how the doctrine of the Trinity can affect life and faith in our churches.

Catherine Mowry LaCugna

Catherine LaCugna is not willing to let the doctrine of the Trinity remain buried and inaccessible as a life-giving gift of the Church to itself. This University of Notre Dame theologian sees the doctrine of the Trinity as essential for a theology of the Church that can produce a healthy and vigorous Church in our time. This is why LaCugna is so troubled by the lack of interest in the doctrine of the Trinity throughout the church today.

She is not surprised at the lack of interest in the Trinity in the church today given the anemic presentation that the doctrine receives in most quarters. A doctrine that is primarily tied up with speculation about the divine inward nature of God in God's self is a doctrine that has been so drained of the power of the experience, life, and witness of the early church that it deserves to be ignored.

For LaCugna the answer to finding new life in the doctrine of the Trinity and putting it back where it belongs in the life of the church is to go back to the roots of its development

Putting the Trinity Back in the Church

in the early church. She believes the ideas present in her understanding of the doctrine of the Trinity were at the heart of the early church's witness. The early church's vitality was not fueled by a concept of God that was happy and at peace with being all wrapped up in God's self. The early church knew a God who was present in their every day. God's wonderful acts of salvation, in Jesus Christ, had changed their understanding and relationship with God for ever.

LaCugna's quest is to de-marginalize the doctrine of the Trinity in Christian theology. She wants to breathe new life into this vital gem of Christian theology.

Though LaCugna would agree with Barth that the early church did not have a full-blown doctrine of the Trinity in hand, she believes the early church's understanding and experience of the nature of God fit the nature of the doctrine of the Trinity that she holds. Their experience of salvation by faith in Jesus Christ and the indwelling of the Holy Spirit that was renewing their lives in Christ's image are all at the root of what she today would call an orthodox doctrine of the Trinity.

The doctrine that LaCugna believes needs to be at the center of the church's life is a Trinitarian doctrine that finds its source in God's act of salvation as revealed in the person of Jesus Christ and the activity of the Holy Spirit.[31] As LaCugna puts it so well,

> In Jesus Christ, the ineffable and invisible God saves us from sin and death; by the power of the Holy Spirit, God continues to be altogether present to us, seeking everlasting communion with all creatures.[32]

What LaCugna's doctrine of the Trinity does for theology

---

[31] "It requires that we root all speculation about the triune nature of God in the economy of salvation (oikonomia), in the self-communication of God in the person of Christ and the activity of the Holy Spirit." LaCugna, God For Us, 2.

[32] Ibid., ix.

Theological Development

is give a helpful way for people to really understand the nature of God in terms and images that can speak to the questions they are asking. Can the God of creation love Me? Who is in control of this seemingly out-of-control world? Can I change and be the person I want to be, or more importantly, whom God wants me to be? Will the world ever get any better? Is anyone, or anything, in control of this crazy world? Can God forgive Me? Can God know my pain and suffering? How are men and women to find true, honest, just community in this broken world? How can the church be a model for true equality in a world of oppressive relationships and unjust social systems?

Theology should be able to answer these kinds of questions, but a doctrine of God that has God safely tucked away in a divine love affair, no matter how wonderful and complete in itself, can not answer these questions.

Each of these questions can be answered in part in a plain reading of the biblical witness. A New Testament reading of the history of salvation is impressive. The history of a messianic birth, a ministry of justice, friendship, and sacrifice by Christ, and the giving of the Holy Spirit all point to a Christ who loves us with great compassion and tender care.

On the other hand, the witness of scripture presents to us a God in heaven who is sovereign, all powerful, creator of all things, and ruler over the entire universe. The problem is how do these two truths come together?

For most of the history of Christian theology we have not done well in uniting these two ideas about the nature of God. The stress has always been on one aspect of the divine nature of God at the cost of the other. Trinitarian thought has focused primarily on God above, the three persons of God relating to each other in loving harmony. The solace to the church in this view is that by a great mystery of faith we can enter into, and be part of, this divine Trinity through meditation. Like St. John on the island of Patmos we have the ability to rise out of our meager existence and be with God in the divine harmony of love and relationship.

This is all great for some, but not for LaCugna. For her the doctrine of the Trinity needs to present the reality of God as the God of relationship not only in heaven but in our midst.

It is LaCugna's belief that the church's doctrine of the

Putting the Trinity Back in the Church

Trinity has not done justice to the biblical witness. It takes that which is a unified whole as presented in Scripture and separates the immanent Trinity and the economic Trinity.[33] This does such damage to the image of God as revealed in scripture that what is left cannot even be called Christian theology.

At its worst the doctrine of the Trinity, as understood by most people, is one that goes no farther than to explain the relational nature of God in heaven. At its best, the doctrine of the Trinity is a double doctrine of immanent trinities and economic trinities which are held apart. This ineffective view of the Trinity had its birth in the fourth century but still plays a real part in the Christian community today.[34]

Karl Rahner can speak of our knowledge of the immanent Trinity revealed to us in the economic Trinity. "In the Trinity in the economy and history of salvation and revelation we have already experienced the immanent Trinity as it is in itself."[35]

LaCugna is not satisfied with the notion that saying the imminate Trinity is the economic Trinity and the economic Trinity is the imminate Trinity. Her agenda is to take this understanding of the relationship between the immanent Trinity and the economic Trinity one step farther. For LaCugna there is not a distinction between the so called two natures of the

---

[33] Leonardo Boff includes these helpful definitions in the back of his book on the Trinity. <u>Immanent Trinity</u>: The Trinity considered in itself, in its eternity and perichoretic communion between Father, Son and Holy Spirit. <u>Economic Trinity</u>: The Trinity as it reveals itself in the history of humanity and acts with a view to our participation in the communion of the Trinity. Leonardo Boff, <u>Trinity and Society</u> Paul Burns, trans., (New York: Orbis Books, 1988), 238.

[34] "Eventually, however, the doctrine of the Trinity became concerned with only one side of this framework, namely, the intradivine relationality of God to God, thought of apart from the relationship of God to us through Jesus Christ and the Holy Spirit." LaCugna, <u>God For Us</u>, 13.

[35] Karl Rahner, <u>Foundations of Christian Faith</u>, Trans. William V. Dych, (New York: Crossroad, 1993), 137.

Theological Development

Trinity.

Her notion is that the reason for an expression of God's Trinitarian nature as both imminent and economic is because of the perceived mystery that seems to hide the imminent nature of God. Now if the nature of the economic Trinity revealed in God's acts of salvation lack some part of God's complete nature as hidden in the immanent Trinity, then we do need to find a way to unite the two. If what we "see" in the economic expression of God's nature is not the same in every way with who God really is in God's immanent nature, then we have to find a way, as Rahner did, to bring the two presentations of God together.

The bottom line is that LaCugna does not see any separation in God's nature as revealed in God's revelation in salvation history and the imminent reality of God. She says that the imminate Trinity and the economic Trinity are one in the same.

LaCugna sees the need to seek an orthodox expression of the doctrine of the Trinity that is not a product of our probing into the secret mind of God but a Trinity that grows out of God's own self-revelation in the biblical witness and the mind of the early church faithfuls. This call from LaCugna is to be faithful not only to the Christian scriptures but to the liturgy and the creed of the church. Her call is to develop a doctrine that does not just pay lip service to what the church says in its doxological assertion but to dig deeply into the very nature of God as revealed by God himself.

The strength of the doctrine of the Trinity is that it points to a greater reality than itself. The doctrine of the Trinity has the power to point us to view the true nature of God as involved intimately in the life of the church and its people. This doctrine opens the door to discussion and contemplation about God that is not dependent on our insightfulness but on God's revelation of God-self to humankind.

LaCugna views the doctrine of the Trinity as a kind of icon for humans in understanding and meditating on the nature of God. The doctrine of the Trinity has the power to shape the thought patterns of our religious consciousness. The doctrine of the Trinity in effect is the church's way of understanding the unity of God's nature as revealed in salvation history with God's heavenly communal nature.

Maybe the most important contribution that LaCugna has added to the Trinitarian dialog is a robust application of the work that was begun by Barth. In her book, God For Us, LaCugna removes the old and crusty shell that had been built around the doctrine of the Trinity and breathes into it new life. Using the tools of the theologian, she weaves her way though the hollowed halls of past histories and agendas and comes back with a doctrine of the Trinity that has the power to enliven and bless the church as well as its worship and mission in the world. Her work puts the study of the doctrine of God back in touch with its vigorous roots that we share with the early witnesses. It is in connection with the early Christian's proclamation of experience and faith that the church today can find the voice to speak to today's problems in decisive and meaningful ways.

Dr. LaCugna makes this statement in the introduction to God For Us:

> The doctrine of the Trinity is ultimately a practical doctrine with radical consequences for Christian life...The doctrine of the Trinity, which is the specifically Christian way of speaking about God, summarizes what it means to participate in the life of God Jesus Christ in the Spirit.[36]

LaCugna's thesis opens new and very exciting possibilities to the practical work of theology in the life of the Church.

Summary of theological thought

Barth's work was the ground-breaking work in a new modern understanding of the doctrine of the Trinity. Though he creates a new paradigm for thinking about the doctrine of the Trinity and its central role in all theological inquiry, he does not work out the applications of his thoughts in other areas of inquiry. If he had, I do not know that he would have come to

---

[36] Ibid., 1.

Theological Development

the conclusions that would allow the doctrine to have the profound impact it should on the understanding of God's relational nature, broadly affecting the relationships that we in the church have with God, each other, and every other element of God's created order. Barth does not seem to want the doctrine of the Trinity to move us as intimately close to God as the early church understood its relationship to be.

Moltmann does the work of applying the doctrine to broad human concerns. He is far reaching in seeing God's revealed Trinitarian nature as affecting every part of human life. He is not shy in finding in God's revealed nature a model and inspiration for the just and holy relationships required of God's people. He embraces the mystery of God "with us" and God "in us," and we in God. Moltmann finds in the doctrine of the Trinity a clear standard for the nature of all relations. The weakness of Moltmann's presentation of God's Trinitarian nature comes from his preoccupation with creations ability to have such a profound effect on God's actions. Moltmann is so determined to protect humankind from any form of dominance by God that he fails to be faithful to the full diet of the biblical witness.

I find LaCugna's work as a bridge in the gap between Barth and Moltmann's theological insights into the doctrine of the Trinity. She is faithful to the full biblical witness but also works out the application of the doctrine in the life, faith, and mission of the church in the world.

Fueled by LaCugna's presentation of the doctrine of the Trinity, we are ready to proceed in seeing how the doctrine of the Trinity can affect the worship and mission of the Church of Jesus Christ.

The worship of God's people is the real entering into the divine nature of God, or more importantly, of God entering into the life of God's people. The mission of the church is not a human driven activity but an entering into what God is already doing in the world. The possibility of human transformation is not dependent on what we can do by our own will power but rather a taking on of the nature of God as we are invited to participate in the holy Trinity. Worship becomes more than the collective acts of a group of committed and well-prepared Christians, but it is the faith community becoming part of a greater sense of worship as prepared by God from creation. Now the idea of community is something that has a divine origin and intention. Our work to bring down the walls that divide us is really only participating in the greater divine intention for all of creation. Any real acts of reconciliation are made possible by being participants in what God is already doing in creation. Our communities are then a reflection of the very nature of God "in us and among us." This kind of thinking brings new possibilities to situations that we could never hope to create by our own powers and abilities.

Before we move to the second part of this book I want to look at one more recent ecumenical inquiry into the nature of the doctrine of the Trinity.

British Council of Churches: the Forgotten Father

In November of 1983 the British Council of Churches established a commission to see if a doctrine of the Trinity had any relevance for the church in our day. The situation that prompted its formation was the Charismatic emphases on the work of the Spirit in the church and the concerns of an ecumenical dialogue begun by the World Council of Churches. The results of this four and one half year long ecumenical gathering were published in three parts under the title of "The Forgotten Father." They came to some far-reaching conclusions.

After protesting the pathetic role that the doctrine of the Trinity plays in the church today (moaning about the state of the doctrine of the Trinity seems a prerequisite for all Trinitarian studies) the BBC Study Commission on Trinitarian Doctrine Today puts forward a bold and inclusive presentation of the role of the doctrine of the Trinity for the modern church. In the BBC's resulting study papers, they not only seek to revive the doctrine of the Trinity as a primary player in the theology of the church but present an argument that the doctrine is essential in our understanding of everything from Anthropology to worship.

As the church tries to understand the place that the doctrine of the Trinity should play in its theology today, it seems to have leap-frogged from just reviving the doctrine as a source of study to saying that the doctrine must play a central if not *the* central place in our understanding of the Gospel.

Theological Development

Such eminent theologians of this century as the Roman Catholic Karl Rahner and the Protestant Karl Barth have made the doctrine of the Trinity the corner-stone of their theology. Their interest, and that of many other theologians, suggests that the triune God is not merely an intellectual speculation or an optional extra, but the very foundation of our lives as Christians.[37]

The BCC is not unique in its broad application of the doctrine of the Trinity in all areas of life. In their study papers the group explores the effect that a doctrine of the Trinity has on such far-reaching areas as; worship, feminism, politics, anthropology, the language we use for God, mission, sociology, ecumenical relationships, soteriology, eschatology, etc. Others who have begun study in the doctrine of the Trinity have come to similar conclusions about the far-reaching impact of Trinitarian reflection.

Though the BCC's study sees the far-reaching effects of taking the doctrine of the Trinity seriously, they also realize that there is only one starting point for the churches' inquiry into the doctrine of the Trinity.

We begin with the triune God whom we meet in and through worship. If we are not communing with a Trinitarian God in our churches and private prayers then clearly such a God is not part of our conscious experience. *It is supremely through worship, we suggest, that the Holy Trinity is made real to us*; this realization is for Christians everywhere and has nothing to do with theological sophistication or academic knowledge.[38]

---

[37] The British Council of Churches, The Forgotten Trinity, #1 (London: The British Council of Churches, Inter-Church House, 1989), 2.

[38] Ibid., 2.

Putting the Trinity Back in the Church

Summary

In this study, we too must start with worship as the place where we come to meet our Trinitarian God. It is at worship and in prayer (also our worship) that we come to experience the reality of a Trinitarian God in our lives, but the reality does not end in worship. We take this reality of living in this intimate relationship with God into all that we do in the mission of our lives.

The Commission's findings point to a new day for the doctrine of the Trinity when it will "lead to a renewal of worship and a deeper understanding of what it means to be a person..."[39] It is to this end that we move to part two of this book. In part two I will make an in-depth inquiry into the way this new Trinitarian/Incarnational understanding of the doctrine of the Trinity affects the worship of the church.

---

[39] Ibid., back cover.

PART II

THE CHURCH'S WORSHIP

There are many reasons people come to worship each week; let me list a few plausible reasons.

We come to pay our respects to God. It is God who has given us everything we have and so we respond to God's graciousness in acts of worship and adoration.

We come to "plug into God," to get recharged because life is hard and we need a lift in order to get through another week.

We come because the sermon gives us such good advice on how to live our lives; "practical" and "down to earth" are the words chosen to describe the sermon for the week.

We come that we and our children might be exposed to "Christian ethics." It is believed that the church is still a good place to develop right moral behavior.

We come as a part of our civic and family duty.

We come because of the "people" and to be part of the fellowship. We need friends in this world and the church is a wonderful place to develop good, solid, friendships.

We come for the "feelings"; it is an emotional high to hear the wonderful music and you just feel better about yourself after coming to worship.

Putting the Trinity Back in the Church

For some, like me, they come to be a part of the production of worship. Pastors, choir members, choir leaders, organist, worship leaders--we all come to produce meaningful worship. We hope to do something of "quality" that will touch the people and bring glory to God.

As you might agree, we come to worship for these and other reasons. It seems to me, though, each of these reasons misses the mark of what we can and should expect Christian worship to be.

Each week, I stand in front of the people of God at 10:30 on Sunday morning and declare the same proclamation over and over again:

"This worship service is the center of our life together." These are words that I say boldly and with confidence, for I believe it is true that it is only in worship we begin to understand who we are and what we are to be about in this world. It is in worship that we discover or become reminded that we are children of God, part of the baptized community of faith. It is in worship that we find the motivation and the shape of our Christian service. It is in worship that we discover the meaning of grace and experience it in our lives. It is in worship that we experience being part of Christ's community. It is in worship that we experience our theology of the Trinity. It is in our worship that we find the paradigm for what it means to enter into the life of God as promised in the New Testament revelation. Worship becomes the standard for understanding the rest of our lives. It is in worship that we are exposed to what it really means to be human beings as spoken of in the confessions, "What is the chief end of man? To glorify God and enjoy Him for ever!"[1] It is in worship that we expect to come into the presence of God at the table as the expectation of a fuller communion around the banquet table of heaven. It is at worship that we gather as a community knowing our community is united and blessed in ways that far surpass our

---

[1] Constitution of the Presbyterian Church (USA), Part 1, The Book of Confession (Louisville, Kentucky: The Office of the General Assembly. 1991), 7.001.

The Church's Worship

ability to enter into community by our goodness and will. It is at worship we experience the healing which comes by entering into the presence of the one who loves us and sustains us. As you can see, I have very high expectations of what worship can, and should, be in the church today.

The fact of the matter is, I don't believe just any old practice of worship will do. We need to be clear about our redefinition of worship if it is to be most helpful to the Christian community. The definition is not designed to put limits on worship; rather, it serves to open our worship experience to all the possibilities of worship that have been embraced by the expectant faithful in every age.

It should be said that I am not limiting worship as a Sunday morning experience, though I do believe that corporate worship should not be overlooked as the our primary focus of worship.

For me, worship is best understood as an entering into an experience that reflects our Trinitarian Incarnational doctrine of the Trinity. For us to come to worship with an understanding of a Trinitarian Incarnational Doctrine of worship is to come ready to meet God in the most profound, honest, and intimate of ways.

When we hold to a Trinitarian Incarnational[2] understanding of worship, we do not to come to worship expecting to receive only what we have to give nor do we come just to get a lift for the coming week. The idea of meeting with and making new friends as the best thing that can happen on Sunday morning needs to be abandoned as we come to understand the true nature of Christian worship. If you really believe it is a Trinitarian God you come into the presence of each week, then you do not come to observe, but you come to participate, and be caught up in, and transformed by your experience of divine worship.

Worship is not just giving back to God what he has already given to us nor is it just singing songs which inspire. And of course we can not come to worship just to honor God or

---

[2] For the sake of brevity I will use only Trinity in place of Trinitarian Incarnational Trinity, but with this understanding of Trinity implied.

to merely meet our civic duty. Worship is moving into the life and love, the streams of redemption that are at the very heart of who God is and what God does. This model of worship does not allow for the limits put on God when we come "just to get charged up" so that we can fall back on ourselves in living out the rest of the week. Certainly we who "work" for the church can not allow worship to become a good performance simply because planning and leading worship is our job. Trinitarian Incarnational worship cannot be limited by the poor excuse that those who lead worship cannot participate in worship. Our understanding of worship is such that it is not what we do on Sunday morning that matters, but that we enter fully into what God is already doing in God's relational life of love and self giving. Even the worship leader, with all the possible distractions that come with looking after the details of worship, will be caught up in a worship that is not of her/his making but a gift from God of full participation in the worship of divine love and heavenly communion. Because of this understanding of the possibility of entering into what God is already doing in ministry Catherine LaCugna is committed to a renewed doctrine of the Trinity for transforming the nature of our theological study. For this same reason I am excited about the possibilities of a church and its people when they take their creeds and their liturgy to heart in a hardy doctrine of the Trinity. The doctrine of the Trinity invites us to a life that is no longer our own but a life lived in the power and presence of God our creator. Theology that starts with a doctrine of the Trinity as its center will never be impersonal or meaningless. Such a theology cannot help but be practical and life-giving-practical in that a Trinitarian theology has implications for all parts of life and life-giving in that by its nature it must become part of our life.

    The worship that grows out of this theology says that we are not alone in worship but that God permeates the very words, actions, songs, feelings that are part of our worship experience. Worship, built on the premise of a God of love and Holy Communion, is a worship that cannot help but to change lives as it invites folks, along with all creation, into the dance of heavenly fellowship encircled in God's divine love.

    It is the thesis of this writer that worship is to be at the very heart of the life of the church. Worship is the lifeline of the

The Church's Worship

church to being the authentic witness of God's presence in the world. Worship is the hub of the wheel of mission and ministry of the church in the world. It is on this central axis of worship that the church aligns itself in order to be the true witness of the church in the world. Worship is the place where the Christian faithful find themselves involved in the life of the Trinity that can change them, empower them, envelope them, and come alive in them. But not just any understanding and expression of worship can meet these requirements. It takes what we have defined as a Trinitarian Incarnational view and experience of worship to fulfill these requirements of being an alive, faithful, authentic church.

My goal in this part of our study is two fold. First, to look at the ordering of worship and how it works out in the Church and second, we will look at how this understanding of worship is worked out in the everyday practice of the church as reflected in its mission.

The following is a list of assumptions that can be made if we hold to a Trinitarian Incarnational doctrine of the Trinity. We will speak more fully on these topics later in the book. For now we will just list them as a guide for further inquiry and to stimulate our thoughts.

1. A study of the doctrine of the Trinity is an examination of the soterological nature of God. The doctrine of the Trinity reveals to us the way that God is, of how God relates to God's created order as revealed in God's acts and revelation in history.

2. There is to be a realization that the work of the Spirit is of vital importance to understanding the nature of the church and how God works in the church. The church cannot be the Christian church without an acceptance of the daily work of the Holy Spirit to fulfill God's plan for salvation. It is only by the gift of the Spirit that God's people can enter into the relational nature of God.

3. The inner-working of God as Trinity is not a mystery. God has fully disclosed God's nature in acts of revelation: first initiated in an intimate relationship with

the first human beings of His creation, reaffirmed in the divine call of Abraham and Sarah, with the last and finest word coming in God's true nature revealed in the life, death, and resurrection of Jesus Christ. In every way God has been completely forthcoming in revealing his nature as a God of relationship and passionate love. The only cloud of misunderstanding that remains is humankind's inability to comprehend all that has been revealed.

4. Our God is a God of community and in turn the church is to model this community in the church. The reality for the church is that it is the body of Christ and so reflects the body life of God's Trinitarian nature in every way.

5. God has taken his place in history as the one "who was and is and is to come." The church's existence is completely dependent on the fact that God enters into space and time and resides with God's people in every moment of their life together.

6. The Trinitarian nature of God reveals to us a God who is, by God's very nature, passionate about being in relationship. Through God's great acts of redemption, revealed in Jesus Christ, we know a God whose greatest desire is to find a way to bring us back into a just and honest relationship.

7. A Trinitarian Incarnational doctrine of the Trinity reveals to us the possibility of a relationship with God that, through Jesus Christ and the work of the Holy Spirit, invites us to know God in the intimate terms of family, allowing us to speak to God as Abba.

8. The doctrine of the Trinity reveals to us the nature of what goes on at our church on a Sunday morning. Our worship is not our own but it is a participation in the divine and perfect worship of heaven.

9. The understanding of life together in the Trinity lets us

The Church's Worship

see our relationship between each other in the light of what is true in the relationships of heaven (Father, Son, Spirit).

10. The possibility of human transformation is tied to the reality that we can be "found in Christ and Christ in us." The Trinitarian Incarnational model of the doctrine of the Trinity says that God enters our lives to recreate the image of God in us.

CHAPTER 5

THE SHAPE OF WORSHIP

How will we order our worship in the light of a Trinitarian Incarnational understanding of the doctrine of the Trinity? I will begin by looking at the possibility of a biblical model for guiding our ordering of worship. I will then look at worship as a means of defining our theology within the congregation. This will lead us to seeing the effects of this kind of worship on our understanding of forgiveness and the possibility of real human transformation within the context of the worshiping community.

A Biblical Model for our worship
    John Peterson challenges us to look at the shape of our worship not in terms of what is expedient but what is God given.
    In his book, <u>Engaging with God</u>, Peterson presents a model for worship that is guided by Scripture. In his study he finds that not only is the Old Testament sacrificial system a foreshadowing of how God deals with his people through the work of Christ but it is a pattern for all of worship.

> ...we need to take seriously the extraordinary biblical perspective that acceptable worship is something *made possible for us by God*. Of special

significance in this regard is the Old Testament teaching about God drawing near to Israel so that his people might draw near to him. The New Testament points to the fulfillment of these ideas in the person and work of Jesus Christ. Again, the Old Testament teaches that the sacrificial system, which was given by God to be the means of dealing with the problem of sin and maintaining covenant relationship with his people, was only effective because of his promise and his gracious enabling. Such teaching finds important expression in the New Testament focus on Christ's death as the means by which we are sustained in the eternal relationship with God.[1] (italics author's)

It is Peterson's thesis that the form of worship revealed to us in scripture is one where God is not only the initiator of worship but also sets its terms, the means of worship. We are inclined to say, if it works, if it draws people, if it has strong psychological underpinnings, it is appropriate for inclusion in the worship service. Peterson does not believe this is true.

To be faithful in our Christian worship we need to be instructed by the biblical witness which reveals to us the terms on which God has called God's people to worship.

We first see the development of worship in the sacrificial system of the tabernacle cultic. It is in the sacrificial system that the people of God can find the means to acknowledging God's kingship. It is in the sacrificial system that a protocol is established by which Israel was enabled to approach the Holy One and to live in the creator's presence.

The relationship that is made available by the sacrificial system is further developed in the giving of the Ten Commandments as recorded in Exodus. Here we see Israel's relationship with their God is not to be at the level of the

---

[1] David Peterson, <u>Engaging with God: A Biblical Theology of Worship</u> (Grand Rapids, Michigan: William B. Eerdmans Publishing Company, 1992), 19.

The Shape of Worship

mysterious and the irrational. The relationship of people and Creator is to be personal and moral.

The worship of God's people is established by God in order to bring them into the experience of what it means to live as God's people. The worship service is to be a time when the people are brought close to God, as well as with each other. The service is also designed for the worshippers to reflect on the nature of what it means to be God's people. The language, the style, the experience, should reflect a greater reality of what it means to be in relationship with the God of creation. This includes acts of homage to God, prayers for one another and the world, experiences of grace, and lively involvement with the greater worship of all heaven.

Peterson sees the New Testament's presentation of worship to be an extension of what was revealed in the Old Testament. The New Testament witness presents the life and ministry of Jesus as a continuation of the covenant relationship established by God with the Israelites. In the New Testament Jesus becomes the new covenant that makes real the sacrificial system of the old covenant.

In the book of Hebrews Jesus is presented as the embodiment of the Great High Priest of the old sacrificial system who has become the true worshipper who leads his people in Christian worship.

The book of Revelation speaks of a lively interaction between the worship of heaven and earthly worship. The writer of Revelation introduces us to the wonderful possibility of entering into a worship experience that joins our earthly voices with the praise and joy of heavenly angels.[2]

Just as the worship we witness in the Old Testament is directed by God, so our worship today is still under the direction of God. The sacrifice and service become inherent in the actions of worship in the Old Testament; what the people were doing with their bodies was also what they were to do in

---

[2] "With the qualification that Christian worship means more than singing hymns in church on Sunday, it is correct to assert that 'in its innermost meaning primitive Christian Worship was intended to be parallel to the Worship of heaven.'" Ibid., 277-8.

their hearts. It is still true today that we are to be guided in what actions of worship are appropriate in our worship. The details have to be worked out in the context of the times, but I believe we do have direction to include confession, baptism, communion, song, scripture, proclamation, and prayer with the over-riding guide being: "worship on earth as it is in heaven."

What Peterson is saying about worship really supports a Trinitarian Incarnational view of worship. Christian Worship, for Peterson, is an archetype of the worship of heaven, a celebration of God's relational, giving, loving, freeing acts of salvation, in Christ, through the Holy Spirit, for all creation forevermore.

Peterson comes to the conclusion that if we are to grasp the authentic nature of Christian worship, we need to depend on the doctrine of the Trinity to lead us in our understanding of what is going on when we worship.

> Through the ministry of the Son and the Spirit, the Father obtains true worshippers. Thus, the doctrine of the Trinity lies at the heart of a truly Christian theology of worship. Each person in the Godhead plays a significant role in establishing the worship appropriate to the new covenant era.[3]

As presented in the opening illustration of this book, this is not the prevailing understanding of the nature of worship. Our relationship with God can be so misunderstood by us humans. We are so ready to make our relationship with God like all our other relationships. We are not surprised at all that God would reject us on terms of our behavior or that we can find favor with God only when we are "good." We have often sent mixed messages about the nature of God. It seems clear that if we are to restore an orthodox understanding of the doctrine of the Trinity as the center of our Christian Worship we will need to be consistent in our presentation through worship, and the theology we teach.

---

[3] Ibid., 285.

The Shape of Worship

Teaching Theology Through Worship

I read a thought-provoking article which contained an analysis of some of the ills of mainline denominations today. In its analysis it looks at reasons why almost all of these churches have been declining in membership for the past 20 years.

In their analysis of those who have dropped out of the mainline churches in the past generation they find that,

> "The underlying problem ... is the weakening of the spiritual conviction required to generate the enthusiasm and energy needed to sustain a vigorous communal life. Somehow...these churches lost the will or the ability to teach the Christian faith in such a way as to command their allegiance. ... If the mainline churches want to regain their vitality, their first step must be to address theological issues head-on." [4]

The reality is we are not teaching much theology in the church today. We seek to "win" people back to the church but we are much more inclined to meet them on their terms, to present a palatable message. When we do teach doctrine, it is more likely the doctrine of conservative lifestyle and politics (i.e. family values) than it would be the classic doctrines of a particular tradition. What we think about abortion or ordination of gay and lesbian men and women seems much more important in how a church defines itself than theological traditions held by a denomination.

The issue is not just teaching doctrine in a class setting, but to take advantage of the doctrine that is already so much a part of our worship: the creeds, the hymns, the celebration of the sacraments. These can all be very graphic and effective teaching moments.

The sacrifice that is so real to people in the breaking of the bread, the grace of God "choosing us" in the baptism of an

---

[4] Found on the internet on CompuServe in the Worship Conference Room.

infant, the bold affirmation of "fully God, fully human" in the creed--these are all powerful and lively presentations of the doctrines of our faith.

The doctrine of the Trinity is one of the key doctrines of the church which has always had a prominent place in the language of the liturgy but has been abandoned as to any practical application or attention.

I find the need for teaching and celebrating the Trinity helpful, even necessary, in guiding the church to understand the full nature of God for us. An orthodox understanding of doctrine of the Trinity can be an effective guide in framing a full and meaningful understanding of theology that touches the needs and experiences of our lives. A Trinitarian Incarnational model of the Trinity gives us a full and balanced understanding of how God loves us and comes to us and lives within each person and we in God.

The Christian faith is not just an affirmation that God is all powerful, or Jesus is kind, or the spirit can fill us with energy. A Christian Theology says all these images stand together. This is why we must renew our interest in a doctrine of the Trinity which encompasses all the vigor that we found in the understanding of the nature of God in the early Church. A Trinitarian Incarnational presentation of our understanding of God brings all the pieces together; it presents the real glory of the faith, that we have a God who made us, saves us, is always with us, one God with many faces of grace poured out for all creation.

Worship and church life can certainly get caught up in all the social aspects of being the church, the fellowship, the marvelous friends, the wonderful feeling of being together. All these will fade with time or in conflict. Even a great love for Jesus is not enough when we still find ourselves hiding from the "Big God" of justice. Our salvation is tied up in a huge picture of salvation that is painted with the big and dramatic strokes of creation, incarnation, salvation, redemption, friendship with God, justice, abiding presence. This wonderful picture is the one that a redeemed doctrine of the Trinity can instill in the life of a congregation.

The teaching of the doctrine of the Trinity seems particularly relevant in seeking a balanced and healthy church in

The Shape of Worship

our day. The tendency of many churches is to emphasize only one dimension of the nature of God revealed in a Trinitarian understanding of God. The "progressive" church stresses the role of God as creator who calls us into relationship with all peoples and all creation as an act of justice and solidarity. The "evangelical" church seeks to share a message of a personal relationship with Jesus that reforms us personally. The "charismatic" church seeks to put people in touch with God's Holy Spirit as a source of power and true worship.

The beauty of the Trinity is that it reveals to us a view of God that balances each of these important aspects of God's relationship with us. When we teach the doctrine of the Trinity as our primary way of understanding the nature of God's relationship with us, we give God's people a tool which embraces God in God's fullness as revealed in Scripture and the early teaching of the church.

We also find in teaching a Trinitarian Incarnational model, as our understanding of the doctrine of the Trinity, the means to fit the language of our liturgy with our theology. Our theology now has a place for the language of baptism and the benediction, the Lord's Supper and Trinity Sunday.

As Barth made the Trinity the hermeneutic of his study, so it is appropriate that we in the church make the doctrine of the Trinity the center of our study of theology and the guide for our worship. The doctrine of the Trinity has far reaching possibilities in expanding the minds of Christian people. The doctrine, rightly taught, has great things to say about people's relationship with God. It explains so much about the nature of the sacraments: how God can enter into our lives, how the Lord's Supper can be an act of participation in the community of God, the nature of being baptized into the Family of God.

The doctrine of the Trinity becomes for us an icon of the real and pervading nature of our God as revealed in the biblical witness.

By making the doctrine of the Trinity a focus for our theological inquiry and the guiding principle for worship, we build a foundation for understanding the nature of God in both experience and intellect. The doctrine of the Trinity then becomes our litmus test. Have we stressed one aspect of the Godhead over another and in the process limited our understanding of God? Are we seeking to accomplish things in worship that do not conform to our understanding of the nature of worship? Though we might not directly "teach" the doctrine of the Trinity, we do use it as our guide to developing and guiding worship.

When we are able to present people with a consistent approach to understanding the nature of God, we help fight the ambivalence that so many people feel about theology. An orthodox approach to the doctrine of the Trinity is not a lifeless doctrine reserved for scholarly theologians but, understood correctly, has the ability to enliven the worship and mission of the church. We in the church must find ways to connect the language of the liturgy with the language of theology in ways that give people a deeper understanding of what it means to be in relationship with God.

I have found great help in understanding the nature and effects of the doctrine of the Trinity in Andrew Roublev's icon depicting the Holy Trinity. This icon painted by this Russian painter in 1425 has been the source of a great deal of discussion in the recent study of the doctrine. Anthony Kelly in his book The Trinity of Life begins his discussion of the Trinity by referring to the impact of Rublev's icon on his feelings about the doctrine. Kelly is very concerned that his thesis on the Trinity not get off on the wrong foot like so many others. It is so easy to limit talk about the Trinity to "abstruse philosophical analyses of highly formal dogmatic pronouncements."[5] He describes his insights into the icon thus,

> The whole thing breathes loving communion, for the fundamental movement of this representation of the Trinity is circular. It suggests the divine communion as a open circle, enfolding the believer and creation into itself...Rublev thus evokes a sense of the Trinity as approachable `from within', in a kind of `inside knowledge', made possible through

---

[5] Anthony Kelly, The Trinity of Love: A Theology of the Christian God (Wilmington, Delaware: Michael Glazier, 1989), 1.

The Shape of Worship

participating in the Trinitarian love sustaining and transforming the world."[6]

Kelly's observations closely parallel my experience in meditating on Rublev's icon. The beauty of the icon is that it draws our attention to a relational understanding of the Trinity and not the typical problems of how three can be one and one can be three (Trinity treated as a problem of higher math).

Catherine LaCugna opens her chapter in the book she edited, <u>Feeling Free</u>, with a discussion of Rublev's icon, finding in it a wonderful insight into the nature of the Trinity she seeks to put forward. Rublev's icon graces the cover of all three of the books that came out of the BBC Study Commission on Trinitarian Doctrine Today. This icon is the first icon to be studied in Henry Nouwen's book <u>Behold the Beauty of the Lord: Praying with Icons</u>. This Icon also is on the cover of Jean Corbon's book <u>The Wellsprings of Worship</u>. It is no accident that all of these theologians chose to give Rublev's icon such a prominent place in their study of the doctrine of the Trinity. To understand the doctrine of the Trinity properly is to allow it to reveal to people the wonderful, relational way God comes to us and stays away from the mathematical models that are usually used.

A study of Rublev's icon sets the tone for the way we need to approach presenting the doctrine of the Trinity in the church today. The path to bringing the doctrine of the Trinity back into favor in the church is full of potholes. The deadly history of the doctrine has created an atmosphere where even the mention of the word creates a mental block in most people which is very hard to overcome. For the most part, this doctrine needs not so much to be taught as to be allowed to inform and guide those who shape and lead worship.

Teaching Forgiveness

As I stated in the opening of this book, solving of the problem of people's understanding and accepting God's forgiveness is at the heart of my need to write this book. How

---

[6] Ibid., 2.

can people under-stand the theology of forgiveness in a truly Christian way?

We cannot understand the nature of forgiveness and atonement without recognizing the vital place that the incarnation plays in bringing about a renewed relationship with God. We also cannot really understand forgiveness in its deepest sense without understanding the triune nature of God. It is when God, in Jesus Christ, is seen and experienced as both the great physician healing our deep wounds and the one, fully human, in need of healing that we can understand the depths of God's ability to forgive us and make us whole.

The incarnation stands right in the middle of bringing about a right relationship between humankind and God. James Torrance puts it this way, "As High Priest, Jesus Christ represents God to men and represents men to God in His own person."[7]

It is the very nature of God to send His Son to us as an act of love to seek us out and call us from sin and into his holiness. I love the powerful way that Balthasar describes what God does for us in Christ, "These (the suffering of Christ) are the redemptive paths of love as it traces the footsteps of sinners in order to catch up with them and bring them home."[8]

It cannot be overstated that the sending of Christ to bring us home was not an afterthought of God. The writer of Ephesians was fully aware of God's choosing of His own even before the beginning of time.

> Blessed be the God and Father of our Lord Jesus Christ, who has blessed us in Christ with every spiritual blessing in the heavenly places, just as he chose us in Christ before the foundation of the world to be holy and blameless before him in love. He destined us for adoption as his children through Jesus Christ, according to the good

---

[7] J.B. Torrance, Theological Foundations, 350.

[8] Hans Urs von Balthasar, Prayer Graham Harrison, trans., (San Francisco: Ignatius Press, 1955), 35.

The Shape of Worship

pleasure of his will, to the praise of his glorious grace that he freely bestowed on us in the Beloved. (Ephesians 1:3-6 NRSV)

It is in the Son that we find the true nature of God's love for us revealed. It is also in and through the Son, by the power of the Spirit, that the love of God for God's children can be consummated in our own son(child)ship.[9]

It is only in Jesus Christ that we really understand fully the nature of God. Christ was fully divine and everything about him reflected the character of God. "He is the reflection of God's glory and the exact imprint of God's very being..." (Hebrews 1:3 NRSV)

As we understand the atonement in the light of the doctrine of the Trinity, we do not see Christ as our benevolent benefactor who stands up to a harsh and overly demanding God. Instead Christ becomes to us God's self, reaching out to us in love and compassion to save his created ones. Christ then becomes our window into the nature of God's love for us. Calvin understands that until God was revealed in Christ our eyes were not able to comprehend God's love for us.

> ...so that we may learn that God is revealed to us in no other way than in Christ. The radiance in the substance of God is so mighty that it hurts our eyes, until it shines on us in Christ ...while God is incomprehensible to us in Himself, yet His form appears to us in the Son.[10]

---

[9] "But the manifest truth of the Father is the Son. In the Son, the Father contemplates us from before time, and is well pleased. It is in the Son that the Father can predestine and choose us to be his children, fellow children with the one, eternal Child, who, from the beginning of the world, intervenes as sponsor for his alienated creatures." Ibid., 51.

[10] John Calvin, Calvin's Commentaries: The Epistle of Paul The Apostle to the Hebrews and the First and Second Epistles of St. Peter William B. Johnston, trans., (Grand Rapids, Michigan: Wm. B. Eerdmans Publishing Company, 1963), 8.

Christ does not only reveal God to us by his nature but, in becoming fully human, Christ now presents us human beings to God. "Therefore he had to become like his brothers and sisters in every respect, so that he might be a merciful and faithful high priest in the service of God, to make a sacrifice of atonement for the sins of the people." (Hebrews 2:17 NRSV)

In the act of Christ becoming a human being, taking on our human nature, he provides the means, as the first born of many children, to make a way for us back to God. He has opened the door for our adoption as sons and daughters and brought us back into the family of God as full participating members. Again it is Calvin's understanding that the real indwelling of Christ in our lives makes justification by grace possible.

> "It is not only that He sanctified us inasmuch as He is God, but the power of sanctification lies in our human nature, not because it has it of itself, but because God pours into our nature the whole fullness of holiness so that we may all draw from it."[11]

But again, it is hard for most people in the Church to understand what it really means to be forgiven. We believe forgiveness is something that comes from what we do. The bottom line for most is that our goodness or our love or our ability to please God is all that allows us to be forgiven, to receive forgiveness, to be worthy of forgiveness. Deep down inside we know it is not right between ourselves and God and something has to be done before it can be made right, to bring us back together. All of our experience tells us this; it is how it has always been and ever will be. So how do we get it straight, how do we make it right, how can we be forgiven by God so we can share company again?

It is in worship we can best present the truth about forgiveness to the people of God. It is as we find a new

---

[11] Ibid., 26.

The Shape of Worship

experience of forgiveness to replace our nagging sense of guilt that we are able to understand what it means to be truly forgiven. It is only through the work of the Holy Spirit in worship that we can truly know what it means to be forgiven by God and so able to enter into our new relationship with joy and thanksgiving: the kind of joy and thanksgiving that not only enlivens our lives but the whole world.

The work of worship, then, is to bring people into a place which allows them to experience the fullness of the love of God revealed in all its glory through the work of Father, Son, and Spirit. We cannot do this on our own but only when we are guided in our worship, or more aptly put, when we enter into Christ's worship. It is only when we are "in Christ" that we can meet the requirements of worship as set forth by God. "...yet as the Incarnate Son, He is the One who worships the Father for us and with us."[12]

James Torrance reminds us again of the real secret of our ability to worship in a way which allows us to truly meet God. It is only when we enter, by faith, into the worship Christ leads us in that true worship is practiced.

In Stewart and Berrymann's book Young Children and Worship, they present a model for Christian education that relies on a worship experience to teach children about God.

> First, the intent of worship is to experience and praise God. While the experience of God in worship leads to knowledge of God, the primary mode of knowing is by participation. God is experienced as we enter into scripture and allow the Holy Spirit to convince us of the truth of God's word.[13]

It is through their experience of teaching children that

---

[12] J.B. Torrance, Theological Foundations, 351.

[13] Sonja M. Steward and Jerome W. Berryman, Young Children and Worship (Louisville, Kentucky: Westminster/John Knox Press, 1989), 13.

they have found that what we know about God must first be experienced before it can be explained in theological terms. This is true for children, all God's children.

It is by the miracle of the incarnation, of Christ's becoming like us, that we can know a relationship with God that is free from the barriers of sin and guilt.

The conclusion that we come to then is that we cannot find the grace of forgiveness and atonement on our own but only through faith in Jesus Christ to act for us and in us. James Torrance says it this way; "He gives my life back to me, converted and regenerated in Him."[14]

It is in worship, which reveals a Trinitarian Incarnational experience of God, that God's people are able to know true forgiveness. It is as we enter into the worship of heaven led by the one true worshipper, Jesus Christ, that we can experience the true rewards of forgiveness as laid out by the gracious actions of God.

The Possibilities of Human Transformation
The ultimate goal of the church is to enter into the worship of heaven. If heavenly worship is the goal of the Church, the primary business of the church is to assist in the creation a people who can join in that worship and, subsequently, the mission of the church which grows out of our worship.

By saying the goal of the church is to enter into heavenly worship is not to say that the ambition of the Christian is to escape into another realm of being. It has always been the conviction of the church that it is possible in our earthly life to experience a life that is so wrapped up in God that it is no longer just our life that we live but a life found in God. By the work of the Holy Spirit we are able to enter into a new relationship with God that is so all-encompassing that it has the ability to transform us into "new creatures all together" with the past finished and gone. At the table, at the baptismal font, we experience a new understanding of who we are and what our lives are to be about. We become part of a greater reality than we have known before. Our eyes are opened to life in the

---

[14] J.B. Torrance, Theological Foundations, 354.

The Shape of Worship

Kingdom of God. We are invited, through the witness of Christ and the summons of the Holy Spirit, to enter into the life of the Holy Trinity. It is as we experience this new life, residing in God's relational nature, that we are transformed into the new people of God. Transformed, not for our own selfish gratification but in order that God might use us, as he has Christ, to bring about God's will for all creation.

No more do I say these things about the nature of transformation than I realize this is not the practice of the church in our day. Though the church knows the biblical language of heavenly transformation, it has often lost its nerve in believing this transformation quality is as powerful or as life changing as it should. If the church and its leaders really believed and acted upon its theology of the doctrine of the Trinity, it would certainly change the way we do ministry.

We have lost our courage in proclaiming the transforming power of true Christian worship in people's lives. We need to believe again that Trinitarian Incarnational worship has the ability to transform lives and conform them to the image of God. The primary tools of the pastor are not the counseling couch or didactic preaching but assisting the people of God in entering into the worship of heaven and so entering into a new life in God. Oliphant Old in his thoughtful study of reformed worship states that worship is the central place where we are created into the body of Christ and transformed into the image of God in Christ.

> It is here (in worship) that we are united together into one body by God's Spirit that we are made participants in the coming kingdom. It is in worship that we hear the good news of our salvation, that we are saved from our sins and transformed into the image of Christ. [15]

Paul Hoon in his book <u>The Integrity of Worship</u> speaks clearly and conclusively when he makes this statement about the

---

[15] Hughes Oliphant Old, <u>Guides to the Reformed Tradition: Worship</u> (Atlanta: John Knox Press, 1984), 8.

goal of worship, "... The end of all our worship is that we should be transformed into Christ's likeness and that he should be formed in us." [16]

This is no new idea for the church; it is just that the church has been taken in by the lure of more seemingly practical, modern, and measurable means for the changing and renewal of people's lives. The limits of all these other "devises" for transformation is that they are all subjective, only therapeutic in nature changing a person's perception but doing nothing to really change a person's state in life. Transformation which is arrived at by entering into a new relationship with God through the redeeming work of God through Christ, made real by the presence of God in the Holy Spirit, makes for an objective change in our lives. We now have a new, renewed relationship with the God of our creation. We are made right with God, "a living sacrifice, wholly and acceptable to God."[17]

An orthodox, and so hardy, doctrine of the Trinity makes claims of possible transformation which far exceeds the hopes and dreams of most pastors in effecting the lives of their parishioner for divine good.

It is in entering into the life of the Trinity that folks are transformed into people who can live in the Kingdom of God with integrity of purpose and action.

Again, it is my contention, that it is only in and through worship that we can bring people to a place in which they can begin to experience and understand what it means to be a

---

[16] Paul Waitman Hoon, The Integrity of Worship (Nashville: Abingdon Press, 1971), 111.

[17] Richard Foster in his work on human transformation through the use of Christian disciplines points out the difference in subjective and objective changes in people, "It is the ground upon which we can know that confession and forgiveness are realities that transform us. Without the cross the Discipline of confession would be only psychologically therapeutic. But it is so much more. It involves an objective change in our relationship with God and a subjective change in us. It is a means of healing and transforming the inner spirit." Richard Foster, Celebration of Discipline (New York: Harper and Row, Publishers, 1978), 126.

The Shape of Worship

participant in the life of God's Holy Trinity. It's not as though I am trying to say that God cannot work this mystery in people's lives in any way God sees fit, but from all that we have discussed, we must come to the conclusion that Divine Worship is God's chosen way of encountering God's people with the possibility of life lived in the family of the Trinity. It is also apparent that it is in this holy experience of the Trinity that God transforms God's people into Christ's likeness and through this transformation allows them to enter into the work of Christ in the world. This transformation is not limited to an inward change within people but in this transformation they become new people "in Christ." As Paul can say, "it is no longer I who live but it is Christ in me."(Galatians 2:20 NRSV) The Biblical language that we spoke of in an early chapter of being "in Christ" is the language which makes human transformation into God's likeness possible.

It again must be emphasized that the goal of this transformation by God is not to our own ends. We are not transformed to meet our own needs or desires. Such a selfish transformation would not be the result of God's work but of other forces contrary to God's desires. True divine transformation can only result in a person who is better equipped to enter into God's saving, redeeming work in the world. Weber states that from the very beginning the Church has understood itself as entering into the work of God in this way,

> "This transformation first takes effect within the worshiping community, which may be called the Eucharistic community. The vision of the earliest Christian community is one of a people who take the social implication of the Eucharist seriously."[18]

With this understanding of human transformation in mind we can see the primary role of the pastor is leading people into a service of worship which allows them to enter into

---

[18] Robert Webber, Worship Old and New, 189.

Putting the Trinity Back in the Church

Trinitarian Incarnational Worship. Making possible worship which allows folks to experience the reality of Christ with us and in us by the power of the Spirit and so entering into the life of the Trinity must be the goal of all worship leaders. This is not something we can control but it is a promise we can accept by faith. Those who design and lead worship must understand how powerful and effectual worship can be in transforming lives. To this end they must try in every way possible to present a worship service that gives people every opportunity to understand and enter into Trinitarian Incarnational Worship. Paul Hoon might call this "pastoral liturgy,"

> ...if edification "does not take place here (in worship), it does not take place anywhere." Despite temptations to managerialism, the pastor is not wrong in seeing the relation between worship and the congregation's life, and (she)he is entitled to be concerned that worship be "pastoral liturgy" in the sense that it strengthen and transform all their life.[19]

Leading worship, with these possibilities in mind, reveals that this work is the most important activity to which a pastor can be involved. In this profound activity of worship, difficult theological doctrines are understood, healing takes place, and people find themselves in the hands of God's transforming power. This work cannot be seen as secondary for the pastor but deserves the worship leader's greatest attention. Worship that calls people into a relationship with a Trinitarian God is at the very center of the work that the pastor has been called to do as she/he seeks to serve the people of God.

A New Approach to Worship
When I get up in the morning my tendency is to make a list of the things I am going to do today. There is so much to do; I need to get a jump on the day if I am going to get it all done. I need to make myself slow down if I am to first listen to God.

---

[19] Hoon, The Integrity of Worship, 27.

The Shape of Worship

There are a number of reasons I can think of that drive me to start the day making "my list."

For one, I have allowed the world to set my agenda. What is important, what needs doing, how I do it are all reactions to the things that my culture has told me I need to do.

My agenda is ego driven. Most of the frantic pace of my life comes from a desire to prove myself. A full calendar, a long "to do list" makes me feel important and worth while. I like it when someone looks over my shoulder at my calendar and comments about how busy I must be.

I am trained to evaluate myself by what I do and what I accomplish. The measure of a person is a full calendar and an impressive résumé.

Eugene Peterson says this ego driven self-worth mentality is easily transferred to the life of the church.[20]

Goal setting in the church is largely influenced by the need to be successful, to look good. A church with a full menu of programs and a great choir, a church which is growing in numbers and budget seldom questions its goals or direction.

Trinitarian Incarnational worship should free us from ego driven goals and directions both personally and corporately. It should change our frantic pace to accomplish for our own satisfaction and redirect us into doing the things God would have us do. Worship should lead into a life where God is the center and not self.

Trinitarian Incarnational worship presents to us a new reality in our lives. The goal of the Christian is not to "prove her or his self" but to seek to enter into what God is doing. The nature of worship, as revealed by God, is not something we create; it is something that is already going on, God's doing, and we only have the pleasure of entering into the ongoing process of worship. If worship is not what we do, but what God is

---

[20] These are comments Peterson made in a Doctor of Ministry class at Fuller Theological Seminary in October, 1990. His premise is that the church needs to set its goal from the viewpoint of its Eschatology. The end should pull us into the future that God has in store for us. Most goal setting in the church is really only an exercise in ego appeasement.

doing, then Christian worship can be defined as any time the people of God become aware of the communal, worshiping nature of God in their world. The real work of those responsible for leading folks in worship is allowing people to be open to the presence of a relational God in their lives. The bounds of worship then need to be enlarged to include all of life for the Christian. Anytime, anywhere, anybody can enter into worship by being aware of God's presence in our lives. To know we can enter into the relational nature of God as part of the Divine Trinity is to enter into Christian Worship.

This leads me back to my getting up in the morning. Instead of getting up to make my list of things to do, I need to enter the morning trying to listen to God. I need to begin my day, alert to the presence of God in worship and open to entering into what God is doing. This "entering in" is not limited to my feelings but is a real process of becoming part of the body of God, revealed in Christ and made possible by the activity of the Holy Spirit. I enter the day, aware of what God is doing in my life and in the world. I move into the day, seeking not only God's will but God's real and abiding presence in my life.

If this then is the true nature of worship, what is the role of those who are charged with leading worship?

I find that Sunday morning worship, with all that is going on, is a difficult place to learn about being attentive to God. It has been my experience that creatively-led services, not necessarily on Sunday morning but ideally in smaller groups, can help introduce people to a Trinitarian Incarnational model of worship.

It is my own experience that it has been at camp, around a campfire, or in some other "special" service of worship that I have understood more fully, or even for the first time, the entering into nature of worship. Times where there can be more quiet, more contemplation, are important places for realizing the true nature of worship as revealed by God. I do not just mean times of "high emotion" when we really think we "feel" God. Worship is not about playing on our emotion or a cheap high. The reality for me is that in these meditative, quiet times, I am better able to see that worship is not our desperately trying to get it done but rather an act of being attentive to what God is

The Shape of Worship

already doing in our lives and our world.

It has been through the practice of small group worship that I have introduced our high school students, to an entering-into worship that better allows them to be attentive to God and what God is doing. This small group worship is not to take the place of Sunday morning worship but is meant to prepare them for what to expect and look for on Sunday morning. These experiences of small group worship invite them to approach all worship looking for what God is doing. The goal is to get them to come to worship, not full of themselves, but waiting on God, listening for God, expecting that they can enter into the great mystery of worshiping in Christ each time they worship.

I have been part of a weekly Wednesday morning worship service with adults that has been a place of worship which in its simpleness has had the effect of allowing folks to encounter God in a different way. Again, this has been a service that encourages waiting on God, not as much acting on our part but waiting for God to act, to be more aware of what God is already doing.

It seems that the church has many opportunities to make places for people to come into an encounter with our living, triune God. I have found the work that Jerome Berryman and Sonja Stewart are doing with children and worship to be very insightful about how we all can learn about the nature of Trinitarian Worship.

Stewart and Berryman have developed a unique program of Christian education for children. Their approach centers on the act of worship believing that childhood is not a time of just preparing for real worship but a vital time of real encounter with God through a worship experience.

The program they have developed rests on the belief that children are ready at a very young age to engage in worship; it is just the styles that need to change to accommodate their particular abilities. Building on the work of Sofia Cavalletti, Stewart and Berryman replace the traditional Sunday school class with worship centers. The centers are carefully planned to allow children to en-counter God through the stories of the bible. Each story that is to be experienced has a set of figures representing the characters and scenes which are part of the story. The class time begins as the children enter the room gently and quietly. Each child is greeted and when everyone has arrived a liturgical song is sung. The leader then proceeds as they go to a shelf to retrieve the box that contains the objects that are part of the morning's story. The story is told simply as each of the objects are placed in position for the telling of the biblical narrative. Their time of worship stresses the story and the figures as the center of attention and not the leader. The story time concludes with each child choosing an activity which allows them to reflect on the feelings that the story has evoked in them. This can be using art materials or playing with the story materials themselves. The worship service then proceeds with the lighting of the Christ candle as the bible is opened and the children are allowed to see the passages from which their story came. The worship time ends with a "feast" that transforms the nursery school snack into a celebration of Christ's resurrection day, a sacrament. The children are dismissed with a personal word to each of them affirming their gifts for ministry in the world.

The beauty of this service is the way the children are allowed to reflect on what God is doing in the stories and then entering into the stories as they become real to them. This is a wonderful express-ion of Trinitarian Incarnational worship at its very best. It is not what we do, not our planning or even our stories that are the focus of worship, but quite clearly it is what God has done and is still doing which becomes the center of their worship experience. The goal of this worship for children is defined by Sonja Stewart as, "The rhythm of the order of worship in the worship center enables children to experience the meeting of God in a way that they themselves can experience, anytime, anywhere, in corporate or personal worship."[21]

I think we have a great deal we can learn about teaching worship to all age levels from this model.[22]

A small group of adults gathered in the sanctuary one

---

[21] Edith Bajema, Worship: Not for Adults Only (Grand Rapids, Michigan: CRC Publications, 1990), 29.

[22] This model of worship is well documented in the Sonja Stewart and Jerome Berrymann's book Young Children and Worship.

The Shape of Worship

Wednesday night. The service they came to was one which encouraged quiet, meditative worship. The only directive by the worship leader was "no talking" (for a change). The service opened with music and then continued with the reading of the scripture passage of the day. After more quiet reflection, the worshipers were invited to enter the scripture story through a guided meditation on the passage. They were invited to pay attention not only to the story but to themselves. How did they feel about Peter's failure, how had they failed?

The service continued with the invitation for worshipers to come forward and light their own candle from the Christ candle. This was a moment for their own personal commitments and reflection on the call of God, through Christ, to them. The service ended with the singing of a song and a benediction.

The purpose of the service was not to be an end in itself but to prepare folks for what to expect as they come to worship, be it corporate or personal.

Summary

Worship is not something we do in trying to present ourselves to God. The act of Christian worship is becoming aware of the worship in which God is already engaged. God's worship is a joyful, life giving, celebration of love and community to which we are invited to join. When we come into the sanctuary to worship we enter into a place in which Christ is already engaged in worship. The worship described in the book of Revelation, of all creation giving praise and honor and glory, is the worship into which we enter.

Through our theology, our style of worship, our words and actions, we need to invite the children of God into an experience of worship that recognizes worship for all it can and should be in the life of the Christian. There is no bad service of corporate worship, there is no person unworthy of participating in the sacraments, there is no rationale which can keep us from experiencing the divine grace that is made available to all creation if we understand and experience Trinitarian Incarnational Worship. As C.S. Lewis says "there is now nothing that separates us from God!"[2]

CHAPTER 6

THE PRACTICE OF WORSHIP

We move now from the ordering of worship with its biblical, theological and practical underpinnings to the actual activities which make up the worship service. We will look at how our Trinitarian Incarnational understanding of worship will affect our theology and practice of preaching and the sacraments.

Preaching
What effect does a Trinitarian Incarnational model of worship have on preaching in the church? There are a number of important implications.

The preacher has the power, by the words she/he uses and even by the unspoken messages they send, to paint a fresh picture of the world in which the Christian lives. This is a new world not limited by the confines put on a life by the limits of the five senses or cultural sensibilities. This is a life that is being redefined, by the nature of God's life "with us" as revealed in Jesus Christ and empowered by the Holy Spirit. It is a life that knows the possibilities of living in the reality of God's relational-Trinitarian nature. Preaching can be one way in which the people of God are invited to live within God's Holy Trinity. I am intrigued by the way William Willimon describes the possible effects of preaching when we get it right. "The best of our preaching has a kind of playfulness about it when in our speaking we invite the congregation to strip down, dive in, splash about, and see what God might make of us."[1]

Preaching, at its best, can open new doors for folks to enter into a real and alive relationship with their God. The preacher reports on the already complete work that God has accomplished in Christ on our behalf and invites folks to enter into this new relationship.

Walter Bruggemann in his book <u>Finally Comes the Poet</u> speaks of the preaching event as a means of creating new possibilities where no possibilities had existed in the past. For Bruggemann the work of the preacher is to voice the reality of the gospel; that something has changed with the coming of the Christ. The preacher is to speak a bold and promising new word which paints new possibilities for the living of our lives in the bright light of the Gospel. Brueggemann sees the preacher giving back to the people of God the gift of "blessed communion," of helping folks to understand the reality of an intimate and life-changing, relationship with God. The preacher connects the deep longing of human hearts with the promise of "God with us."

> "To live in blessed communion" is a serious and central promise of the gospel; one day blessed communion will be the destiny of the faithful. One of the reasons people show up on Sunday morning is this inarticulate yearning and wishfulness for a lost communion. We are not sure how or when it was lost, but we sense the loss. Nor do we know much about reentry and access into the fellowship. There is, nonetheless, a yearning. That yearning is the hope of the congregation, and the task of the preacher is to bring to speech that deep yearning. In that

---

[1] William H. Willimon, <u>Peculiar Speech: Preaching to the Baptized</u> (Grand Rapids, Michigan: William B. Eerdmans Publishing Company, 1992), 32.

The Practice of Worship

speech the preacher also dares to respond from the other side; to speak for the God who has authorized and evoked the yearning, who yearns as we do for another beginning. The preaching moment occurs in the midst of this terrible loss and this resilient hope. Our speech in the context of loss and hope affirms who we are and what has been promised among us.[2]

Brueggemann sums up the role of the preacher in one line, "The preacher is charged with speaking the word that permits new communion."[3]

The sermon then becomes, in a sense, a sacrament. As the Lord's Supper reveals the real presence of God with us through loaf and cup, so the sermon should reveal God's presence in words and images. Paul Hoon sees preaching and the Lord's Supper as both affecting the worshipper for the same end result but through different senses.

> What goes on in preaching is precisely the same thing that goes on in sacrament, and sacramental feeding is the same kind of feeding as that which preaching, praying, and meditation provide: "The sacrament does not differ in essence from any other spiritual exercise. Just as preaching 'putteth Christ into our ears' so the sacrament puts 'Christ into our eyes, mouths, hands and all our senses."[4]

Preaching can open our hearts to the almost unbelievable possibility that God has entered our world and invites us to Holy Communion. In preaching we can reveal the possibility of

---

[2] Walter Brueggemann, Finally Comes the Poet: Daring Speech for Proclamation (Minneapolis: Fortress Press, 1998), 43.

[3] Ibid., 49-50.

[4] Hoon, The Integrity of Worship, 107.

Putting the Trinity Back in the Church

entering into the realm of God's relational nature spoken of as the doctrine of the Trinity. Preaching is the proclamation of a reality, though hidden from the wisdom of the world, is revealed in God's history of salvation.

Everything in Trinitarian Incarnational worship points to the possibility of living in communion with God. Worship is an invitation to rethink our understanding of how the world works. Worship invites God's people to experience life in the spirit. Worship takes people from the place of depending on their own goodness for salvation to entering into what Christ has done for them in finding reconciliation with God. The act of preaching in the worship service should attest to the fact that we can come to know and experience God, as an active participant, in the divine relationships of heaven. We are no longer outsiders, wishfully admiring the love revealed in the heavenly Trinity, but we find ourselves on the "inside" experiencing all the joys and privileges of life lived with and in the family of God.

As I preach I feel as one reaching out, with the loving-embracing arms of God, to bring folks back into a relationship with God, a relationship which has the power to change their lives for eternity. The Preacher in some ways acts as a temptress, using words and images to entice the people of God to believe again a story that is too good to be true, a reality that is the only true source of a fully functioning life.

This does not necessarily limit the styles or forms of preaching. Most of the time the doctrine of the Trinity is not overtly spoken of in the sermon. What a Trinitarian Incarnational style of worship does is lay an infrastructure for the appropriate content of the worship service.

The idea of a "how-to" sermon can run counter to the goals of Trinitarian worship. How to raise a Christian family, how to be a good dad, how to cope with depression, all have the tendency to call people to depend on what they can do to make their lives better. This approach to preaching can feed folks' desire to do it themselves, because no one else will. James Torrance warns the pastor not to be "throwing people back on themselves" but to keep reminding them of the redeeming nature of the Gospel as revealed in the work of Christ.

Preaching can declare the demands on a life lived under the lordship of Christ, but it must never be proclaimed outside

The Practice of Worship

of the context of grace. Preaching can join in the celebration of an earthly family of God in the life of the church but it must never allow that family to be seen as a means to true salvation.

To give people even a hint that their salvation can be achieved through the use of brain power or will power or great desire or a community of wonderful friends, is to warp the nature of God's saving work in God's world. We humans wish that it was by our own doing that we could find a right relationship with God. Our reflex is to seek out redemption through our own doing. This is a lie that we dare not encourage in our preaching.

Our preaching should always be pointing to the reality that it is only "in Christ" that we have a sure promise of being found in God for eternity. Christ is our salvation, our true humanity, our justification, our righteous relationship with God. It is only in Christ, by the power of the Spirit, by the gracious compassion of the Father, that we find ourselves intimately embraced in the community of love that is named the Holy Trinity. Preaching is to voice this gospel truth in ways that allow folks to take the first step of faith of trusting the promises God made in the mighty acts of salvation history.

Preaching then works hand in hand with all the other elements which make up the worship service. More than this, preaching helps define, and reflect on all of life. Preaching helps make sense of the way God can be, and is, involved in the everyday events of our lives. Preaching is to encourage refection on how the stories of scripture are the stories of our lives. Preaching at its best is an invitation, by word, by mood, by gesture, by attitude, by inflection, into the greater reality of a life lived within the relationship of the Holy Trinity.

There is a warning I must make about the pitfalls of preaching. Preaching must never be allowed to be diminished to another form of personal manipulation. Preachers do not shape lives; God does. We are not in the business of molding people in our image, we are in the business of pointing folks to God.

Preaching can easily become just one more means by which we try to motivate people to believe the way we do. In preaching we are not to press our agenda, no matter how righteous we feel it is; we are to introduce folks to a relationship with God. We share a relationship that is so caught up in the life of God, as revealed in the doctrine of the Trinity, that their lives will reflect the goodness and will of God. As our only true worship is worship initiated and made possible by Christ, so the only way to lives acceptable to God is to live lives made possible by the sacrifice of Christ. God made Christ to be the first born of a new humanity born to bring glory to the Creator. We find our lives made acceptable to God as they are found hidden in Christ. Our one true priest takes us to God in himself, forgiven, redeemed, and made new. Preaching should respect the mighty power of God to transform lives. Preaching should point to a greater reality in which the long held misconceptions of a people lost in a world of despair and hopelessness can find new hope in a life truly lived "in" God.

The preachers' only acceptable message is that God can and does transform lives and we are invited to participate in that life. It takes an act of faith, on the part of the pastor, to believe God is sovereign and fully capable of transforming lives. It takes an act of faith for the preacher to believe that God can work in the lives of those who think very differently than she/he does. It takes an act of faith on the part of the preacher to believe that God can take care of God's own, that living in the reality of the Holy Trinity really does transform folks to an image and lifestyle acceptable to God.

God is the one who is active in the preaching event. Those who carry the message are only players in a much bigger plan that God has already put in place and continues to act on every moment of every day. It is not preaching that changes lives; it is people moving into God's lively Trinitarian presence, a place of grace, redemption, salvation, justice, and new life.

The Sacraments

There are two moments in the life of the worshiping Christian community which stand out as moments when we gain new understanding of what it is to be brought into the family of God's Trinitarian life. Baptism and the Lord's Supper are key to a Trinitarian Incarnational understanding of worship.

Baptism

The Practice of Worship

The sacrament of baptism in the reformed tradition is a wonderful expression of how coming into the family of God is not something we do but is purely dependent on the grace and love of God. To bring an infant to the waters of baptism is to say that God chooses us before we even know the words to choose God for ourselves.

On the one hand, baptism is the time when we experience coming into a new relationship with God as a child in the family of God. At baptism we gain all the privileges and responsibilities of being a member of this family in every way through the work of Christ active in our lives.[5]

At the same time, we are brought into a new family that is realized in the local church. It is this new family which makes vows to support and love the new family member. These are not vows that we hope to keep on our own, but by the grace of God working in us as the baptized community brought together by God.

Baptism is a wonderfully important event in the life of a worshiping community. Baptism is one of those moments when we see and celebrate the Trinitarian worship of heaven among our very own, the God of creation, celebrating the life of his child, by the power of the Holy Spirit. If Christ's baptism is our baptism, then baptism is not only our entrance into the church family but also into the life and experience of a Trinitarian Faith.

The images of baptism are a rich source for our understanding and experience of what it means to live in Christ. This is why Martin Bucer, the leading Reformer of Strasbourg, was particularly concerned that baptism be performed as part of the regular worship of the Christian congregation rather than as a sort of private service conducted for the family.

---

[5] "It was through baptism that Jesus entered into the kingdom of God and it was through baptism that the disciples followed Jesus into the kingdom. Even today it is in baptism that we too enter into the kingdom of God. Baptism is a prophetic sign at the beginning of our Christian life that we belong to the people of God. It is our entrance into the church." Hughes Oliphant Old, Guides to the Reformed Tradition: Worship, (Atlanta: John Knox Press, 1984), 9-10.

Putting the Trinity Back in the Church

The teaching quality of public baptism came home for me not long ago. At the end of a baptism service one little boy was overheard saying: "I want that for me." All the teaching in the world could not have had the same impact on that little boy as those few brief moments in worship when he realized the draw of the kingdom of God for him.

Our reformed understanding of baptism has wonderful possibilities of education and transformation in the lives of our children and adults. With our tradition of infant baptism we make a number of powerful theological statements. In infant baptism we state that God loves this child and in some way adopts this child as God's own. When my four year old foster child speaks of his baptism he calls it "the day that God adopted me." The affirmation is that God chose us and brought us into a relationship that is likened to that of God's relationship with his child Jesus. We understand this act in the light of Jesus being baptized by John in the Jordan. In Christ we hear again the words of our Holy Parent when God says "this is my beloved 'child' in whom I am well pleased." In our baptism we are made one with Christ as Children of God.

This understanding of the importance of baptism for grasping our relationship with God was played out for me in a particularly poignant fashion in an encounter with a member of our congregation.

She is a woman who over twenty years ago was part of a community that committed a series of hideous murders. Leslie has been incarcerated in a women's prison for the past twenty-four years and has little chance of ever being free again. Leslie was baptized at Village Church when she was a child but left the church in her early teens as she got involved with a 60's cult.

In contacts with her mother, I came to visit Leslie regularly. By her invitation we began talking about how God could love her after all she had done. After many visits we set up a worship service in the prison chapel. In this service of worship we sang the songs of Leslie's youth and read the familiar scriptures she grew up with. We then celebrated a service of re-affirmation of baptism where I preached on the baptism of Jesus in the Jordan and finished with making a sign of the cross on Leslie with water from Village's baptismal font and saying "remember your baptism and be thankful, in the

The Practice of Worship

name of the Father and the Son and the Holy Spirit." This was a powerful statement to Leslie of who she is and to whom she belongs. At the heart of her being she is not to be defined by the acts of her youth but by the fact that she is a child of God and in her baptism she was chosen by God.

I believe this is the lesson all of our children need to know at the very heart of their being. At every baptism performed in the church we are making a declaration that, in and through Christ, we are incorporated into the life of God revealed in God's Trinitarian nature. We, like Christ, are made part of the great reality of God's relational existence. Like Leslie, God's children are not defined by what they have done, or have not done, but ultimately they are defined by their relationship with God. God has chosen them. The world would choose to define people by throwing them back on themselves. Your accomplishments, your mistakes, your athletic proficiency, your disabilities, are the things that cause us to see who we are by the limiting standards of the world. In the Church we declare that we are not ultimately defined by these things. We see ourselves clearly only when we see ourselves through the eyes of God. We know our true selves only as we participate in the Holy Trinity of Love.

As in any family, being members of God's holy family includes blessings and responsibilities. As we are grafted into God's family tree we receive an inheritance which now defines who we are in tangible and intangible ways. Not only do we carry the name of Christ but we are indwelled with life of Christ. Christ "in us" changes who we are and how we act and how we feel. The biblical witness promises that "in Christ" we are a new creation. It is as though we have a new genetic make-up infused into our bodies. The renewal of God's image in those chosen by God is intangible by scientific measurement, yet a real event in the life of the Christian.

To carry the name of Christ brings the responsibility of honoring Christ and the one whom sent Christ. The family that the Christian is united with is a family of the highest values and moral standards. These values and standards go beyond any superficial worldly standards replete with ulterior motives. The values of the Holy Family seek justice at all cost, are always aimed at redemption, and never falter. These are the family values which every Christian takes with them into the world that they serve in the name of their God.

This is the family, the Holy Trinity, to which Leslie is called and grafted. This is the dynamic relationship of God's loving ways to which all Christians are invited to share.

It is in baptism that we recognize this profound reality of being found in God's family, to be incorporated into the divine Trinity. I have found that the church does not seem to understand or cherish the sacrament of baptism as it could. This sacrament is such a blessing to the church I have sought ways to lift up baptism as a defining event in the life of the church.

Reaffirmation of Baptism

In trying to bring baptism back to the center of the church's declaration of its self-understanding, we have introduced the service of Reaffirmation of Baptism as introduced in the new Book of Common Worship of the Presbyterian Church (U.S.A.)[6]

It will be helpful to share some of the background of the reaffirmation of baptism service that is being used at village Church. It was about two years ago when we introduced a reaffirmation of baptism service which we now celebrate twice a year. We were very careful in introducing this service because of concern that this practice might be seen as a rebaptism service. Before we introduced this event for the first time I wrote an article in our newsletter about the nature of this service and the precedents for it. In the service we took great pains to make it clear what we were doing and made it clear people did not have to participate if they did not feel it would be helpful.

At Village this service has become very important in making the sacrament of baptism central in defining who we are. The water of baptism is the sign of our entrance into an intimate relationship with God. We are invited, through the sign of this sacrament, to believe ourselves truly part of the Holy Family. In a church where we have few infant or adult baptisms, and when we do the show is easily directed away from God's work among us to a display of "cuteness," the

---

[6] Book of Common Worship (Louisville, Kentucky: Westminster/John Knox Press. 1993).

The Practice of Worship

reaffirmation service clarifies the role of Baptism in defining the nature of the church and its people.

If baptism defines the start of our new found relationship in the life of the Trinity (and it does) then participation in the Lord's Supper exemplifies what it means to be a person who lives continually in the life of the Trinity.

The Lord's Supper

The celebration of the Eucharist is unparalleled in its ability to communicate to the people of God a sense of God's Trinitarian nature and their part in its reality. It is at the table that we can appreciate what it means to join in a holy relationship with God. It is at the table that we can appreciate what it means to join in the worship of heaven. It is at the table that we can best understand what it means to be a family of God, united in the community of God's outreaching love.

It is in John Calvin's development of his doctrine of communion that we find his most profound statements about the nature of living in the realm of the Kingdom of God. Calvin had no problem believing that at the table Christ was truly present. He goes even beyond this in saying that it is also a reality that when Christ joins us at the table in our earthly sanctuary we also join him at the table of the wedding feast of the Lamb.

Again we find in our sacraments the supreme understanding for a Trinitarian faith. What God had promised to Moses at the burning bush, "I will be with you always", is now acted out in the ministry of Jesus and attested to by the Holy Spirit as the covenant is sealed.[7]

Worship on earth as it is in heaven is not an act of wishful thinking or illusion to Calvin. It is at the Table that we no longer count on our goodness to be reconciled but only on the grace of Christ working for us and through us and now with us.[8] The Lord's Supper becomes a time when God's people can

---

[7] "It is by sharing a meal with him that the Covenant is sealed." Old, 134.

[8] "But the essence of the sacramental action consists in the "actual conveyance of spiritual meaning and power by a material process...not

gather around the table of grace and experience what it means to be part of a Holy Family. We are not invited to gather around the table when we finally get things right or we are at last good enough or when our works are pure. We come to the table with all that might keep us from God hidden in Christ's goodness and transformed by God's grace. By the gift of the Holy Spirit we are made one with the Trinitarian Family of God. A key to understanding the nature of Communion is seen in who is invited and eventually comes to the Holy Table.

Children and the Lord's Table

I believe welcoming children to the Lord's Table is a natural and required action of a church that practices infant baptism.

To invite our children to partake in the mystery of God's grace in baptism without including them in the continued blessings of God bestowed at the Lord's Table does damage to the whole idea of Christian community and the nature of how we are integrated into the blessed communion of God's presence.

For our children to be excluded from the table sends a message that they are less than full members of the family. To exclude our children from the table does great damage to our understanding of how we are engrafted into the Trinity of Heaven. How can we exclude our children from the table because of lack of understanding when we ourselves can never hope to understand, in this life, the full meaning of this wonderful mystery, this act of mercy? If it is Christ who makes us family in our baptism, who are we to exclude any baptized member of the church from the family table?

I think bringing our children to the table as soon as they are able to understand eating and drinking is a wonderful sign of the great power of God to make us a Family of God in spite of ourselves. And more than a sign, having our children join us at the table is required of those who believe that our primary relationship with God is based on a new relationship with God

---

only God's meaning to the mind, but God Himself to the whole person of the worshipper." Underhill, Worship, 43.

The Practice of Worship

revealed in a life lived in the reality of God's Trinity. It is at the table that we celebrate a new relationship with our God. It is at the table that we come together to celebrate and experience life lived to its fullest as promised in the witness of the salvation history. It is at the table, and only at the table, that we can become family as God intends family to be.

Bringing children to the table, with the whole family, reveals to all that the Holy Table is the place for redemption and new relationships. This "open" table of God's love and relationship is spoiled any time any one is excluded. The Holy Table, set by God, is our finest representation of what life should, and can, be like. Any time we put our limits on who can come to the table we are doing great damage to how we model the true nature of God's love to the world.

The Worship of all creation

As we work out a Trinitarian Incarnational practice of worship we come to an idea that is less tangible than the preaching or sacraments but needs to be very evident in the shaping of the service.

On Sunday mornings our invocation is often the singing of the hymn "Earth and All Stars." This song brings to our realization once again the nature of God's un-surpassing redemption of his created order.

> Earth and all stars, loud clashing planets,
> sing to the Lord a new song.
> Earth wind and rain, loud blowing snow storms, sing to the Lord a new song.
> He has done marvelous things,
> We will sing praises with a new song.[9]

I believe that we don't really understand the joy possible in worship until we understand the place that the rest of creation has in our worship of God. It's as we speak not only for ourselves but for all of creation that we can enter into a worship experience that truly reflects the joy experienced in heaven.

---

[9] Presbyterian Hymnal #358

Paul sets the stage for this incredible act of rejoicing when he describes the waiting that had to take place before joy was revealed.

> We know that the whole creation has been groaning in labor pains until now; and not only the creation, but we ourselves, who have the first fruits of the Spirit, groan inwardly while we wait for adoption, the redemption of our bodies. For in hope we were saved. Now hope that is seen is not hope. For who hopes for what is seen? But if we hope for what we do not see, we wait for it with patience. Likewise the Spirit helps us in our weakness; for we do not know how to pray as we ought, but that very Spirit intercedes with sighs too deep for words. And God, who searches the heart, knows what is the mind of the Spirit, because the Spirit intercedes for the saints according to the will of God. (Romans 8:22-27 NRSV)

I very much agree with J.B. Torrance when he describes just why worship in its fullest sense can be so powerful. It is because of how we were made.

> But God made man in His own image to be the Priest of creation, to express for all creatures the praises of God, so that through the lips of man the heavens might declare the glory of God, that we who know we are God's creatures might worship God and in our worship gather up the worship of all creation.[10]

A Trinitarian Incarnational understanding of worship leads us naturally to this wonderfully full and joy filled place of worship.

For one, it puts us in a place where we could not go on

---

[10] Torrance, Foundations for Ministry, 348.

The Practice of Worship

our own. It is only as we enter into what God is doing in God's great work of salvation of all things, in heaven and on earth that our mission as God's people is fulfilled. It is only within the Trinitarian nature of God that we can hope to enter into the worship that includes all of the created order. It is a gift of participation in the life of God in all its fullness that we can know such joy in the worship of God.

Secondly, it is only as we enter into the realm of being one in Christ, and so brought into the experience of God's Holy Love revealed in the Trinity, that we can have the compassion for the "birds of the air and the trees of the field," even the rocks that "cry out," for redemption to join them in their own call for salvation. It is only in the experience of what we have called "the trinity" that we can hope to learn to sing in harmony with all God's creation.

How can our joy, for all that God has done for us in Jesus Christ ever be put into words? The end result, it cannot. There is a wonderful moment in the communion service when the worship leaders proclaims: "And now we join with all creation as we sing together saying..." the time when we most exemplify the goal of the Trinity, as everything in heaven and earth is caught up in praising God. "To glorify God and enjoy Him forever." This is not just the chief end of humans but the chief end of all creation. It is only in a Trinitarian Incarnational doctrine of the Trinity that this image, of all creations praising God together, makes any sense. And it is only when the end goal of all worship is a joining together of all creation in praise to God that we are truly practicing Christian worship.

Summary

Though worship is intended to be the starting point of where the people of God begin to understand what it means to be the Church Christian worship also leads God's people into a life of mission defined by their worship experience. The transformation of being invited into the life of God's Trinitarian nature creates a new creature who now lives a life that exemplifies the love and life of God.

In part three of this book I will look at how a Trinitarian Incarnational view of worship should shape the mission of the Church. I believe that this new look at the doctrine of the

Putting the Trinity Back in the Church

Trinity has very important implications for the way the church conceives its mission to the world.

PART III

THE CHURCH'S MISSION

"The New Testament conception of worship as the unity of *leitourgia* and *diaconia*, of worship and service, must always be borne in mind; surely we cannot call any experience of worship authentic which leaves conduct unaffected."[1] These words of Paul Hoon make the all-important tie between worship and service as a requirement for authentic worship. The liturgy (the work of the people) must not be limited to the people gathered in worship but evident in the people scattered. So it is in worship that we find our motivation for mission. By definition then, worship ties us directly to service and mission.

---

[1] Paul Waitman Hoon, The Integrity of Worship (Abingdon Press, Nashville, 1971) 54.

CHAPTER 7

THE SHAPE OF MISSION

It is only as we know Christ and Christ's mission that we can know the shape and form of our own mission. More than this, it is only in entering into the relationship of the Trinity that we can find any success in carrying our Christ mission to the world.

It should be said that when I speak of "our mission" I mean something more than just mission as it relates to the work of Christians doing church work. Our mission is made up of the task of our daily life. Our mission includes all areas of life: work, family, school, and play. In our commitment to Jesus, every part of our lives comes under the lordship of Christ and so every part of our lives becomes tied to our mission in service to Christ. "For we are God's servants, working together; you are God's field, God's building." (1 Corinthians 3:9 NRSV)

Worship as the Heart of All Christian Mission
We can seek out a mission strategy of our own--we are very capable of that--but then it would have the dubious burden of being our mission and not Christ's. Our understanding of what it means to live the Christian life is not first and foremost in our actions or even in our goals. Our Christian life is revealed to us through a relationship with the living God as revealed by

Christ and instilled in us through the work of the Holy Spirit. It is by faith that we come to know the gracious loving act of God in Jesus Christ, which has the power to make us one with the God of Creation.

Because of the relational nature of our life in Christ we can only know our mission as it is revealed to us in the life of Christ both historically and relationally. Our mission is Christ's mission and Christ's mission is ours. This does not mean we do not use our own intelligence to lead us to an understanding of how mission is worked out in our lives. We are to keep our eyes open to the world around us as we seek our mission in the world, but it is Christ's mission that must inform us about the integrity of our mission endeavor.

In an article in the Dictionary of Christian Theology the author states that the source of Christian Mission is found in the Trinity, "Mission is an activity of God and has its origins in the Holy Trinity."[1] We find it is only when we turn our eyes away from ourselves and look to Christ and his mission that our mission will be truly Christian. "The Church is the instrument of God's mission but it is not the theme of the mission."[2]

When we decide for ourselves what the nature of our mission will be, we also choose the source of power for our endeavors. When we are the source of direction for mission, we will get just as far as our own resources will take us, we are again "thrown back on ourselves." To be a truly Christian mission, we need to enter into what God is already doing in Jesus Christ in his mission to the world. "So in our corporate worship we are called to be a royal priesthood, bearing on our hearts the sorrows and cares and tragedies of our world as our

---

[1] R.M.C. Jeffery, Theology of Mission An article in A Dictionary of Christian Theology Alan Richardson, ed., (Philadelphia: The Westminster Press, 1969), 217.

[2] Ibid., 218. There is a wonderful discussion of the meaning of Mission in this article; of particular importance is the understanding of mission not being primarily concerned with personal salvation but with the larger picture or reconciling all of the created order with God.

The Shape of Mission

heavenly High Priest does."[3]

When we act on our own, our limits are very evident; when we enter into what Christ is doing, there are no limits as to what we can do. "In mission, the disciples were to go out like Israel traveling light, moving quickly and with similar urgency. But the real mission can only begin in the power of the risen Christ."[4]

Worship is very central to our being able to enter into what God is doing through Christ to the world. It is at worship that we are able to become attentive to the presence of God in our lives. It is at worship, in the rich sense of both private and public worship; we turn our attention not on ourselves but towards God and God's presence in our lives. It is as we become attentive to the presence of God in our lives that we can move in faith to trust the work of God's love in our lives. It is God's love, revealed in Christ, which allows us to enter into a relationship with God that also allows us to enter into God's work in the world.

Christ's Mission is both a corrective for our mission (life activity) as well as the source of our mission endeavors. Our mission needs to grow out of a relationship with God which is berthed in worship and prayer. Our mission needs to grow out of our communion with God in order to be Christian Mission and not just "good intentions."

The shape of our mission is more than a model of what God is doing in salvation history. Our mission actually is God's mission in the world. As we enter into the life of the Trinity, we begin taking part in what God has been doing in the world for eternity. Our mission activity is injected with the reality of God's nature. God's mission activity is contagious to those who have been called into relationship in the Divine Trinity of love and redemption. The church and its people catch what God is and we enter into the work of being God's arms of love and

---

[3] J.B. Torrance, The Place of Jesus Christ in Worship, An essay in Theological Foundations for Ministry Ray S. Anderson, Ed., (Grand Rapids, Michigan: Eerdmans Publishing, 1979), 355.

[4] Ibid., 218.

grace to all creation.

The mission of the church, then, reflects the divine love that is the Trinitarian nature of God. As we will find, the shape of the churches' mission will often be at odds with the dominate agenda and goals of the world order.

The Trinity as a model for community

If we find our shape for Christian Mission in Trinitarian Incarnational worship, then, we see a model for our personal relationships that is at odds with the primary model for personhood and relationships in our society. The Trinitarian Incarnational model of worship speaks of an understanding of community that shapes all interpersonal relationships.

The absence of true community in our society today has become a concern of many. Robert Bellah chronicled this lack of community in his landmark work "Habits of the Heart." After five years of fieldwork and interviews the writer(s) of the book came to this startling conclusion, "We are concerned that this individualism may have grown cancerous..."[5]

The concern for the church in this preoccupation with self is what it does to people who have been cut off from the community of faith. It has always been the role of the church to bring people of faith into a community of caring and mutual concern in which the people of God could grow to maturity. James Torrance sees this understanding of people in community as a direct result of the doctrine of the Trinity,

> What is needed today is a better understanding of the person not just as an individual but as someone who finds his or her true being-in-communion with God and with others, the counterpart of a Trinitarian doctrine of God.[6]

---

[5] Robert Bellah, Habits of the Heart (New York: Harper and Row Publishers, 1985), vii.

[6] James B.Torrance, The Doctrine of the Trinity in our Contemporary Situation an essay in The Forgotten Trinity: Vol.3 A Selection of Papers Presented to the BCC Stury Commission on the Trinitarian Doctrine Today Alasdair I. C. Heron, Ed., (London:

The Shape of Mission

The doctrine of the Trinity requires us to see people and the place of community in a different light.

Individuality and American Culture
In Bellah's work we discover that the people of America have lost a sense of need for community in their lives. The foundations of their lives are built on the premise that it is only the strong individual who can be successful and safe.

We come by our deep value of individual independence honestly. It was this independent spirit which allowed the early American settlers to withstand the many challenges that faced them in the initial years of establishing this country.

I can see this in people with whom I come in contact through pre-marital counseling. One partner of many of the couples whom I marry speak of not being raised in any one tradition but (theoretically) exposed to many traditions so that they could someday choose their own expression of faith. It is my experience that the end result of this kind of child rearing leaves a person without an appreciation for what a Christian community (or for that matter, any community) can mean in their lives. Having never been part of a community of faith, they see no need to seek out a community and so never do connect later on in life. It is very frustrating to speak to these people about what the Christian community can mean to them when they don't have any experience of it from their youth.[7]

Bellah's concern is not necessarily individualism as such but a lack of understanding about the place that a community can play in one's life. This leads to a general concern of Bellah for the future of the American people, "Absolute independence is a false ideal. It delivers not the autonomy it promises but

---

BBC/CCBI Inter-Church House, 1991), 15.

[7] The Catholic Church showed their awareness of the powerful draw that an early experience in the community can have in later life when they chose the theme "Come Home for Christmas" as their Advent campaign slogan a few of years ago.

loneliness and vulnerability instead."[8]

As we lose an understanding of the role which a community can play in the life of persons, we cut ourselves off from the very body that shaped who we are in the first place. Our culture is in great danger if its people do not have communities to mold them and shape them and hold them together.

> But the notion that one discovers one's deepest beliefs in, and through, tradition and community is not very congenial to Americans. Most of us imagine an autonomous self existing independently, entirely out-side any tradition and community, and then perhaps choosing one.[9]

The need for intimacy

William Willimon has a wonderful understanding of the role worship can play in our lives and does not claim too much when he states, "Worship is pastoral, edifying, corporate, and integrative."[10]

I believe that being a part of worship in our formative years can have a lasting impact in our understanding of what it means to be part of a community. It is in worship that children gain a sense of being a part of something that is bigger than themselves. It is in the traditions of the church that children can learn the values on which they will build their lives. Bellah believes there are many people who are more indebted to their religious background in building their value system than they

---

[8] Robert Bellah, Habits of the Heart, 247.

[9] Ibid., 65. "The concept that a community can set standards, adopt values, capture conscience, and become authoritative in the life of human beings is not obvious in our culture, and it(culture) falls apart without it." Ibid., 240.

[10] William H. Willimon, Worship as Pastoral Care (Nashville: Abingdon Press, 1979), 21.

The Shape of Mission

admit. The shame of this lack of understanding is that they do not pass on this important tradition to their children.

It is in Christian community that we can find the meaning for our lives that is missing in an individualistic society. It is in a body of faith, realized primarily in worship, which we find ourselves connected to others as well as the one who created us.

Most of the experiences of community in our culture are predicated by our common experiences and needs. The problem of these communities is that they change as our experiences and needs change. This does not constitute true community as a transforming power in our lives. The community that has the ability to do the things that Willimon describes can only be found in a community that has a power vested in it greater than the sum of the participants. The worship that grows out of (as well as forms) the Christian community is worship that enters into the greater reality of worship which is shared with the Father, Son, and Spirit.

As we in the Christian community join in the worship of Christ as brothers and sisters, a Family of God, we experience true community that has the power to change our lives and build a foundation that is greater than anything that we can ever hope to build on our own. The views of the Orthodox tradition are wonderfully presented by Alexander Schmemann in his book, "For the Life of the World."

> They have been individuals, some white, some black, some rich, they have been the "natural" world and a natural community. And now they have been called to "come together in one place," to bring their lives, their very "world" with them and to be more than what they were: a *new* community with a new life. We are already far beyond the categories of common worship and prayer. The purpose of this "coming together" is not simply to add a religious dimension to the natural community, to make it "better"--more responsible, more Christian. The purpose is to *fulfill the Church,* and that means to make present the One in whom all things are at their end, and

Putting the Trinity Back in the Church

all things are at their beginning.[11]

The church, in light of its doctrine of the Trinity, makes the bold assertion that human beings were created to live in community. And in this same doctrine the church discovers the shape of this "new" community. The doctrine of the Trinity defines our relationship with other human beings as well as our relationship with all of creation. The church needs a definition of the Divine Trinity that is radically relational in nature to do justice to God's self revelation. This radically relational Trinity does not limit itself to the realms of heaven but projects itself into the very creation which it sets in motion. This doctrine of the Trinity then requires us to see our own nature, not as a collection of individuals accommodating the necessity of community but as a people and creation which can only find its natural self, as created by God, in the context of community and relationships.

Our understanding and experience of Trinitarian Incarnational Worship leads us to a mission objective that offers to our world a counter view of what it means to be a human being and the nature of true community.

Belonging

I believe that this view of human nature as presented in the worship life of the church explains the strong need in human beings to belong. From our very earliest experiences of living in society we want to belong. My four old foster child had a great need to belong to a family (our family). My fourteen-year old daughter had an almost obsessive need to belong to a peer group which establishes identity and security. My twenty-six-year old daughter is now in the process of building her own family, leaving us to be with the one she loves in another part of the country.

I don't think the people of my family are unique in a deep need to belong to a people who help define who they are and will become. Because of unfair courts and fickle friends and

---

[11] Alexander Schmemann, For the Life of the World (St. Vladimir's Seminary Press, 1973), 27.

The Shape of Mission

even the possibility of divorce, none of these important relationships are substantial enough to support our need to belong. Not even the Christian community as a fellowship and support group can meet our need to belong and be part of something bigger than ourselves. It is only in the Church, at worship, that we enter into a community that is capable of supporting us in our deep need to belong. It is in our joining with all of creation in divine worship that we enter into a community that has the strength and endurance to support us throughout our lives (and then some).

A primary way the mission of the church is shaped by its worship is in the way worship can allow us to participate in community that is not limited by our weaknesses but enlightened by God's life with and in us.

Pastoral Care and the Healing of Souls

The mission of the church is not only shaped by worship but is a direct result of what worship can accomplish in the lives of its participants.

In our individualist society we have overlooked the powerful role worship can play in healing the emotional lives of people. There are few present day psychologists who would see any therapeutic benefit coming from an involvement in a worshipping community. If anything, most therapists would see more harm than good coming from the influence of "religion" on the lives of individuals.[12] The real issue for this book is the fact that this attitude is not only held by the psychological community, but is also the attitude that is practiced in the church. The reality is, we in the church have largely abrogated our role of healing people's deep emotional hurts to "trained therapists" and the secular therapeutic method. We have lost our nerve when it comes to trusting the powerful influence of worship in the healing of souls. Paul Hoon sees the problem but also the solution for the church,

---

[12] I mean "religion" here in the worst possible sense. I would say that lots of counseling that has been done in the name of "religion" is really malpractice and now being called that in some recent court cases.

Putting the Trinity Back in the Church

Many pastors will eagerly acknowledge their debt to the pastoral psychology movement over the past few decades, but a certain uneasy is mingled with their gratitude. Too often pastoral care has been conceived in individualistic and humanistic terms, especially as it takes the form of pastoral counseling. Often it is conducted independently of the Christian community and is indistinguishable from secular therapy. The answer to our uneasy, we increasingly understand, is to recover something of the classical definition of pastoral care as the extension of the same saving and healing Word that is made known in preaching and sacrament.[13]

It is not too harsh a judgment to say that if we really believed what we say we do about the work of Christ in our worship we would never relinquish worship's vital role in the healing of people's lives.

In our desire to behave professionally, the local pastor has often become little more than a referral service for the deeper psychological needs of our congregations. We have succumbed to the pressure to believe that only intense psychotherapy can have any real impact on the deep-seated psychological needs of our people. In most cases, the only real alternative to staying involved in the intimate care of parishioners was to become trained therapists ourselves. This was not always the case for the pastor as Willimon points out, "In an earlier time, a pastor caring for his flock, engaging in the activities related to the cure of souls meant, in great part, leading them in worship."[14]

We should not forget the power that exists for healing in the people who are part of a worshipping community. As we

---

[13] Paul Waitman Hoon, The Integrity of Worship (Nashville: Abingdon Press, 1971), 28-29.

[14] Willimon, Worship as Pastoral Care, 35.

The Shape of Mission

invite people to enter into the mystery of Triune worship we invite them to a place that has the ability to transform and heal lives in ways that we cannot fathom.

This is not to say therapy does not have a place in the cure of souls. There is warrant to believe that the methods of the psycho-logical community do help people grapple with areas of their lives that without this intervention can never be healed. The point is, the church should not turn the handling of psychological illness over to the therapists but must join with them in healing of souls. As we play our part in this healing, our greatest resource centers on the worshipping community that we invite people to join. "Our pastoral care is carried out within the context of a worshiping community attempting to live out its faith in this world. To forget that context in our care is to lose our perspective, our identity, and the source and resource of our care."[15]

Oliphant Old gives good advice when he says: "Let us leave counseling couches to the psychologists and make the service of daily prayer the heart of our ministry of pastoral care.[16]

The impact of the worshipping community is not limited to an hour on Sunday morning. The impact of being part of the Christian community is that we are not only made one with Christ but we are also made one with each other, as brothers and sisters in Christ.[17] In a real sense we are given a new family with Christ as the head when we enter into our new relationship with God through worship.

It is in this new family that we can find a powerful healing for the hurts of our lives. As we invite people to enter into the worship-ing community, we invite them to become part

---

[15] Ibid., 27.

[16] Old, Guides, 176.

[17] In reading Hebrews 2:11-13 we are to be reminded that through the work of Christ we are not only made children of God and brothers and sister with Christ, we are also made brothers and sister with each other in the Family of God.

of a family unit which can fill the deep human need to belong which was never provided for in the family of birth.

It is important that the local congregation understand the important role they can play in healing peoples' lives. For many people it is only in the worshipping community that they find a place where they are able to share the joys and griefs of their lives.

Even for those who have other places to share their joys and griefs worship is still an important place to recognize these events. In the context of worship we see the major events of our lives in the light of a greater reality founded in worship.

> "...but the conviction that the great moments of celebration, fear, grief and mystery in life can best be marked by Christian worship should not be dismissed as sheer superstition or slavery to tradition. It suggests some continuing relationship to the Christian faith and the worship of the church which must be taken seriously."[18]

It is only within the context of Christian Worship that we can discover who we are and to whom we belong in ways that can reshape our lives.

Children and the Worshiping Community

I think we say a lot to our children in our approach to worship. If we act as though we expect things to happen when we come into the presence of God, if we make our personal and public worship a vital part of our lives and show that it is valued and treasured, then our children can believe that being part of a worshiping community will have an important effect on their lives.

In a world that is so threating to our young people an introduction to Trinitarian Incarnational worship can make a profound difference in their growing up. While parents are

---

[18] Duncan Forrester, James I.H. McDonald and Gian Tellini, Encounter with God (Edinburgh: T.&T. Clark Limited, 1983), 2.

The Shape of Mission

looking to the church to promote good moral behavior in their children they should be expecting a great deal more. The work of Berrymann and Stewart show that children have a great capacity to enter into a personal relationship with God. I have found that High School students are more than ready to embrace the mystery of God's Trinitarian presence. These students find services which stress communion with God very inspiring. We must give our young people ample space to encounter God and a vision for relationship with God that is radically Trinitarian. When we do this we give them a foundation for faith that allows for growth. As their mental abilities change, so their concept of God can change within a basic relationship with God. As other values change and they reject the so called "worn-out" values of their parents, their basic understanding and experience of God can still grow in this new sphere of influence.

Introducing our young people to a faith which allows them to enter into a dynamic relationship with God is a much needed gift to our children in these challenging times. When we pass on our faith as a set of moral and ethical standards for our children to observe we risk a rejection of these values. As our values are questioned in our children's ever expanding world we face the possible rejection of not only our values but the Christian faith we hope to pass on to them. When faith is passed on as primarily a relationship with a dynamically relational God, we pass on, not our limited ethical values but the building blocks for creating their own understanding and expression of faith that is true to the environment in which they live.

The Community of Faith

It is by our participation in the nature of the Trinity that we are able to find out who we really are as revealed in our relationship with God. Evelyn Underhill makes this claim about the Trinity "In the light of the Trinity, we discover our true selves."[19]

This new understanding of self in the light of our

---

[19] Underhill, Worship, 27.

relationship with Christ is described with great clarity in 1 Peter and the Book of Revelation, "But you are a chosen race, a royal priesthood, a holy nation, God's own people, in order that you may proclaim the mighty acts of him who called you out of darkness into his marvelous light." (1 Peter 2:9 NRSV) "...and (He) made us to be a kingdom, priests serving his God and Father, to him is glory and dominion forever and ever. Amen." (Revelation 1:6 NRSV)

In this area of "knowing one's self" I believe the church needs to play an important if not decisive role. It is not enough to just know intellectually that we are part of the Family of God. The real joy comes when we experience this knowledge of family and belonging and being loved in ways beyond our limited vocabularies.

Until we experience being a part of the Family of God in a way that can touch our souls, we cannot really know the joy of worship that goes on in heaven.

In most of my new member classes the overriding theme of why people join our church is "because everyone is so friendly." This seems very shaky ground for joining this church or any other church, knowing the fractured nature of the people who make up the church. Though misled, this comment does reveal something about the needs that people have when they do join a church. The people I meet in class are in search of a place where they can find family, a group of people who love them. They want to matter to someone, have people in their lives who will care for them because they choose to and not because they have to.

The fact of the matter is, the people of the church don't have it in them to love people as they need to be loved. We are doomed as a church to fail at being the loving family people need unless the formation of family is built not on our merits and goodness and ability to love but "in Christ" as its head and cornerstone. The family which these people need must be bigger than we are able to be on our own. This can only happen when we are a church that experiences family as proclaimed by the writer of Hebrews, "For the one who sanctifies and those who are sanctified all have one Father. For this reason Jesus is not ashamed to call them brothers and sisters." (Hebrews 2:11 NRSV)

The Shape of Mission

We become a family only by the grace of God working in and through us in Jesus Christ. It needs to become the experience of the community, as they come together in worship, that Christ makes them a family of God blessed by the working of the Spirit in and through them. We become adequate and healing brothers and sisters only as we find our church family, a family created by God.

In baptism we also learn something of the family that God calls us to on earth. It is in the Church that we begin to understand what it means to be a part of the family of God in heaven. It is in this imperfect family that we begin to understand what it means to be a part of God's perfect, loving family in heaven. It is in worship that we celebrate not only our joy in being the children of God but also celebrate that we have a family in Christ to which we belong. This is a very important need of our children and all the children of God: to have a place where we belong, where we know we will be loved, in spite of ourselves.

In the youth new member class one young man explained what it means to be part of the church through baptism by saying: "it means that you have to be loved, because you belong." This was a great assurance to him in a Jr. High world that is not very good at practicing unconditional love.

Doxology and Praise

Before we finish our conversation about the shape of mission, inspired and transformed by Trinitarian Incarnational Worship, we must speak of the place that doxology has in our discussion.

Catherine LaCugna understands that the praise of the church is more than another human act of trying to excite their senses out of boredom. Praise or doxology has the role of allowing us to enter into the relationship of the Trinity in ways that transform us into a people of God. As we enter into praise we enter into something that God is already doing. Praise is God's act of coming out or God's self to enter into the joy of all creation, the coming out of God into the world that we are part of by God's grace.

Praise is the creature's mode of ecstasis, its own

self-transcendence, its disinclination to remain self-contained. The creature's doxology is evoked by God's ecstasis, God's glorification in the economy. Praise is the mode of return, `matching' God's movement of exodus. God creates out of glory, for glory. The return is part of the rhythm of life from God to God. In that communion of love is gathered all religious endeavor. In that rhythm and movement all economic and political life is caught up in a vast communion of shared life, shared goods, shared pain, and shared hope.[20]

Doxology then allows God's people to experience, if only at times for a fleeting moment, what it means to live outside of our own limited perceptions and enter into a world bigger than our own. In the praise of worship we find what it means to be alive as God created us to live. In the doxology, we are given a vision for what we are called to be. When we find ourselves joining with all creation to glorify God in common voice we touch on what it means to be fully human and alive. Be it in a hymn, the sermon, around the table, or in the confines of private prayer, doxology has the power to take us to a place of self expression that joins us to a greater level of praise that is at the very heart of God's being and self expression.

SUMMARY

Though the shape and form of our mission and service is cultivated through worship it should not be overlooked that worship itself is an act of mission. This only strengthens our assertion that the primary role of the pastor is to lead and encourage Trinitarian Incarnational Worship. The worship the pastor leads and encourages has profound effects on the life of a congregation. In worship people come to know life within the Trinitarian nature of God. In worship lives are changed, vision is renewed, people find themselves reconnected to the life-giving source of all life, and hope is re-born. Worship not only

---

[20] LaCugna, God for us, 350,1.

The Shape of Mission

shapes our mission but, in many ways, it is the mission of the church. We do not just come to worship to be blessed and sent out to do the real work of the church. When we come to worship and invite others to the worship, to partake in the liturgy, we find ourselves doing the mission of the church in real time.[21]

We will now look at some of the ways that the practice of mission, shaped by worship, affects people and institutions in our world.

---

[21] "Real time" is an expression used to express something happening now and not with any delay. In our computer era this is an important distinction to be made. So many of the ways we communicate are not in real time. Most everything is delayed by recording. When communication happens in "real time" it is an exceptional event. Worship then in the church is not a means to mission but a real act of mission in and of itself. Happening when it happens, not something we look forward to in a future action.

CHAPTER 8

THE PRACTICE OF MISSION

It is not hard to see that a robust Trinitarian Incarnational understanding of worship will profoundly affect the way the Church views the world and its activity in the world. This experience of worship is seen as God's people being taken up into the work of God's Holy Trinitarian presence in the world. This experience, of being part of God's relational nature, transforms how we see ourselves, it transforms who we are. Entering into the worship of all creation, in bringing glory to God, cannot end at the sanctuary door. This profound experience of entering into work that is so tied up in the will and destiny of God moves us to new acts of service and mission. Our Christ-led worship changes the way we think, we act, we feel, and we live. It is to this new way of thinking, acting, feeling, and living that we address in this chapter.

The scope of this book does not allow us to look in detail at all the implications that a Trinitarian Incarnational worship experience would lead us. This new life, lived in the reality of Trinitarian love and relationship, will affect every area of life. To be part of God's great movement of self-giving love and assertive acts of redemption carries God's people to places of service and understanding that will reshape the world they live in. Our task here is to investigate some limited areas where our understanding of worship and mission will guide our thinking and acting. We will seek to observe the patterns that emerge as we apply our approach of Trinity-led worship to the life of Christian people.

Ecology

At the very heart of a radically Trinitarian view of worship is that worship is not limited to what we conjure up, no matter how inspiring or well thought out. The worship we come to is worship led by Christ, inspired by the Holy Spirit. The worship of God's people encompasses all of creation. When we come to worship we come to an already in-process meeting that includes hills and rivers, animals of every kind, even stones lend a voice as the people of every nation and time lift up their voices in common and glorious praise. We find in our worship a sense of oneness with all that God has created. Our oneness though does not come through a common inherent, nebulous spirit but by a common direction and longing for completion in the Creator.

This view of worship and relationship with God has great implications for a theology of ecology.

It is based on God's passionate desire for redemption of all creation. At the core of our worship is a common voice and common longing for life as it should be, as promised by God. To leave worship only to continue the mindless and selfish destruction of nature makes our worship a farce. Life lived in relationship and solidarity with the reality of a Trinitarian God does not stop at 12 noon on Sunday.

What allows us to dare tackle the ominous and costly task of participating in God's redemption of all creation is that we do not do it alone.

Central to our understanding of Trinitarian Incarnational Worship is that it is Christ who is the one true worshipper. We only find our way to a life of worship when we find ourselves in Christ. It is also true that Christ is the only true "ecologist." The difficulty of the task, the complexity of the solutions, and particularly the cost of faithful and loving acts toward creation make taking proper care of all creation impossibility for mere humans. We are to seek the redemption and salvation of the created order but we are at a loss just as we are at a loss to bring

The Practice of Mission

about our own salvation. So, as we do in worship, we seek to enter into the glorious and faithful work of Christ as we answer the cry of nature for redemption.

The work may be hard and the task beyond our limited capabilities (or even desires) but as we enter into the work that God is doing we know our work will not be in vain but always leading towards a day of completion and success in The Day of Christ.

Racism

I think racism and prejudiced attitudes toward people who are different than we might be the biggest problem facing the church. I see the sin of those who built the infamous Tower of Babel very much alive in the church today. The threat of people who think differently than we, act differently, speak differently, look different, and challenge our way of doing things as we "always" have, is very real in the church.

The story of the Tower of Babel presents the antics of a people who tried to create their own "community" of comfort. In the safe confines of their controlled environment, with the support of their manufactured community, they felt there were no limits to the heights they could reach. The irony is it was not until this counterfeit community was destroyed that real community, as it was intended, could exist.

God leveled this fabricated homogenous community and made possible the establishment of the real divine community that celebrates its creation at Pentecost. The church was born as a community of very different people of different languages, cultures, skin colors, who were brought into a divinely inspired family of God. True community is only obtained as a gift from God.

Today, in our effort to find a safe place, in a world that is so threatening, we have again tried to build our own homogenous community. This contrived community becomes a place where we feel comfortable, where we think we understand each other, where similarity of culture, language, and skin color keeps us from facing the challenge of diversity.

The challenge that an active and alive doctrine of the Trinity presents us with is to see our church community as a reflection and earthly display of the Trinitarian nature that we know God to be.

We now find our community is not to be defined by how we relate or get along. On the contrary, our community is defined not by anything we are, but by the fact that God is head of our community. The most astonishing act of Pentecost was the coming together of thousands of people from every race and creed to become the church, a community, not held together by their similarities but by the grace of God and the activity of the Holy Spirit.

In the power of the spirit, we are called to participate in relationships that redefine what community is. Community is not the place where we feel safe and comfortable, where everyone is alike, the only true community is community created by God.

The table is the place where this community is most fully realized. At the Table of our Lord we are made one not only with God but with each other. The doctrine of the Trinity presents to us a God who knits us together in the church by the work of God's diverse but ever relational nature. It is in this wonderfully eclectic gathering of God's people that we can come to know not only each other but ourselves. In this way the church becomes a place where the walls that divide us come down and the unity of creation, which is God's greatest desire, can begin to be celebrated.[1]

---

[1] "...living as persons in communion, in right relationship, is the meaning of salvation and the ideal of Christian faith...Human beings are created in the image of the relational God and gradually are being perfected in the image (*Theosis*), making more and more real the communion of all creatures with one another. The doctrine of the Trinity stresses the relational character of personhood over and against the reduction of personhood to individual self-consciousness, and also emphasizes the uniqueness and integrity of personhood over and against the reduction of personhood to a product of social relations. Thus it can serve as a critique of cultural norms of personhood, whether that of "rugged individualism" or "me first" morality, as well as patterns of inequality based on gender, race, ability, and so forth." LaCugna, God for us, 292.

The Practice of Mission

Sexism

The idea of Trinity with its language of Father and Son has been a stumbling block for many in the movement to remove patterns of sexism in the church. Though the native language of the Trinity does seem at first to be alien to the cause of those who would thwart sexism, in truth the doctrine of the Trinity presents a wonderful corrective to inappropriate male/female relationships.

The conventional pattern of roles between men and women historically has been for men to dominate over women. Though I had hoped that we were evolving to a place where this is changing, I am taken back by movements in the church today that seeks to reestablish the old patterns of a different "simpler" time. In trying to deal with the rapid change in our culture, they seek to go back to the "good ol' days." This includes supporting a traditional understanding of roles between men and women where the man is head of the household and women are to be subordinate.

As if it is not bad enough that these folks are trying to naively recapture the romanticized past of their parents, these movements insist that they can build their case on the authority of scripture.

What they do not seem to understand is the nature of biblical interpretation. There are revelations in scripture that are meant to be foundational for understanding who we are and what is expected of us. There are passages like "there are no longer male and female, slave and free, jew and gentile" or "for you have died, and your life is hidden with Christ in God," where the clear intent is to point the way to a new ordering of society and relationships in the coming, and more and more realized, Kingdom of God. These are theological passages which speak not just to a culturally isolated situation but to all people in every time and place. These declarations are the building blocks for any theological inquiry into the nature of living life as the people of God.

Then there are passages like "women should be silent in church," or "women should not teach men." The purposes of these passages are not intended to be theological truths for all time. The objective of these directives is to a particular situation with a specific historical context. Not that these directives could not be fitting in another time and place but it is not universal in its application. Kenneth Bailey, as one who understands the culture of the Middle East, does a wonderful job of helping us understand how the cultural setting affected what the Apostle Paul was getting at in these passages.[2]

When looking at God's ideal for relationships in our world, we need to get our guidance from the theological passages that allow us to ascertain how God would, and does, speak to our particular situation. Because the doctrine of the Trinity is built on these passages of revelation, it becomes for us an excellent source of insight for a theological inquiry into the nature of all human relation-ships.

The doctrine of the Trinity points us to the revelation that our God is a passionately relational God. This ardor for relationship is revealed to us in the activity and relationship of the Holy Trinity.

As we have built our case in this book, the Trinitarian nature of God is radical in its scope. Not only are the three persons of the Trinity related in love, but they are inner-related in being. The Father and the Son are one, and the Spirit is the presence of the Son in us, and if we know the Son we know the Father, etc.. We are found in Christ, we too are invited to participate in this radically relational community of Heaven. As revealed to us then, the relationship patterns of the Trinity could not be more in opposition to a hierarchal system of relating one to another.

Christians then must be guided in their relationships by the reality of our invitation to participate in the Holy Trinity. By the power of the Spirit we find ourselves uniquely integrated into relationships with our Trinitarian God and with each other.

The doctrine of the Trinity is not a stumbling block to equal and just relationships between men and women; on the contrary, our understanding of the doctrine of the Trinity

---

[2] Bailey has produced a video series that seeks to see Paul's pronouncements to the church about women in their proper cultural context. When these pronouncements are seen through the eyes of one who knows the middle eastern mind and social structure we see the appropriate application of Paul's teaching to the church.

The Practice of Mission

requires us to challenge any pattern of relationship that does not reflect God's Trinitarian nature.

Catherine LaCugna has done a wonderful service to the church in her investigation into how the Trinity serves as a model and corrective to the way we view the role of men and women in the church.

Politics

As we find ourselves caught up in this Trinitarian relationship within the dynamics of Father, Son, and Spirit we are brought to a new place of understanding ourselves and our role in the world. Being a Christian does not mean being a person who has just changed her/his mind set. What we find when we become Christians is that we are now in the midst of a protest march in which we have joined God in seeking justice and redemption with hearts true to God's desires in every way.

John Calvin found the revelation of God in his life a call to challenge the principalities and powers of his time in the reordering of governments and society. We too find in our relationship with God a call to seek God's justice in the structures of our society.

When we understand, and live out, our new relationship with God we can no longer separate our life in the church and our life in society. The movement of God, as revealed in God's Trinitarian nature, requires us to determine our political stances in relationship to our life in Christ.

Summary

Even this limited inquiry into the implications of the doctrine of the Trinity in all of life reveals the depths that an enlivened and robust doctrine of the Trinity takes us in ordering the Christian's thought and life.

This path of practical application of Trinitarian Doctrine has been where most studies of a renewed doctrine of the Trinity have led.[3] It is the only logical conclusion of a dynamic

---

[3] Most of the theologians we have referred to are interested in how the doctrine of the Trinity affects all areas of a Christian's life. Moltmann, LaCugna, Rahner, Schmemann, Thomas and James Torrance, and Kelly are all modern day leaders in this area.

doctrine of the Trinity to pursue how the doctrine of the Trinity will affect our lives and actions when we leave formal worship to continue our participation in the holy actions of the Trinity in our everyday lives.

The movement from theology to worship to mission to application in the world, is a natural movement for the doctrine of the Trinity as we have defined it in this book. The process of allowing our dynamic relationship with God to permeate every area of life is required if we believe what we say about God. Every thought, every relationship, every decision, every act, must conform to the reality of our new and energetic relationship with God.

PART IV

PREPARING THE CHURCH

American pastors are abandoning their posts, left and right, and at an alarming rate. They are not leaving their churches and getting other jobs. Congregations still pay their salaries. Their names remain on the church stationery and they continue to appear in pulpits on Sundays. But they are abandoning their posts, their calling. They have gone whoring after other gods. What they do with their time under the guise of pastoral ministry hasn't the remotest connection with what the church's pastors have done for most of twenty centuries.[1]

Eugene Peterson is an articulate spokesperson for the need of pastors to return to a classic definition of what pastors are to be doing.[2] Peterson sees the intense pressure on pastors

---

[1] Eugene H. Peterson, Working the Angles: The Shape of Pastoral Integrity (Grand Rapids, Michigan: Williams B. Eerdmans Publishing Company, 1987), 1.

[2] Peterson is an ordained Presbyterian Pastor and now professor of

today to be "productive" and "useful" as measured by standards which are foreign to that which guided pastors for most of the last 2,000 years. This pressure is only heightened by the decline in numbers in all the mainline denominations. A reduced demand for pastors has put these folks in the position of feeling the need to justify themselves even more than in the past. What is the role of the pastor and how can she/he best serve their congregation?

As we have stated many times, the central role of the pastor is to lead the people in worship. This is not the sole role of the pastor but if she/he does not start in worship the rest of their ministry is in grave danger of being distorted and misled. Worship is the place where the people of God have always come to discover what it is to be the people of God, of who they are and what they are to be about.

We now turn to some insights into how a Trinitarian Incarnational view of worship will guide the role of the pastor.

---

spiritual theology at Regent College in Vancouver British Columbia. Peterson's three books on pastoral vocation <u>Five Smooth Stones</u>, <u>Working the Angles: The Shape of Pastoral Integrity</u>, and <u>Under the Unpredictable Plant</u>, should be required reading for all pastors.

CHAPTER 9

THE PASTOR

What are pastors to do? It's as though they are being set up for the marketing pastor syndrome. In the world of limited budgets and hard to achieve worship attendance goals they are inundated daily with programs that promise to bring people into their doors. "The phone's for you" promises to supply the church with hundreds of visitors, seminar after seminar taught their success in reaching the "boomers" and "busters" and "x-ers." The goal of keeping the customer happy and meeting their perceived needs has become the gospel of church growth in the 1990's.

As the church is compelled to meet so many needs, and is pressured to make itself relevant in today's society, how can a pastor find the center in the storm of competing demands? What are the most important things he/she should be doing?

The Role of the Pastor
Our radical Trinitarian view of God, with the trinity seen as the starting point of all investigation of God's nature (and the only true source of a relationship with God) reveals clear guidelines as to how pastors are to approach their task in the church.

Putting the Trinity Back in the Church

Pastors are to be about the business of making people aware of God and how God is working out salvation history. The pastors seek to invite folks to enter into what God is doing in their world.

The Old Testament model for doing this has always been within the worshiping community. The New Testament Church was birthed in an act of worship on what we now call Pentecost. The first century church continued to gather together on the first day of the week, in acts of worship, to hear the Word read and preached, experience the bread broken, to sing praises to God, and pray. It was in worship that the church received its form and discovered its function. Though the early church did not use the word Trinity, it was a Trinitarian view of God that so radically changed the people's understanding of the nature of God.

A Trinitarian view of God opened doors to a new kind of relationship with the God of creation. No longer was God "way up there"; now God was a God of relationship, reaching out, inviting. The way to salvation and wholeness was not bound by the limits of human perfection but made possible through entering into what God had done and was doing in Jesus Christ and it is in the act of worship that the church experienced this reality most profoundly.

If it is the role of the pastor to point people in the direction of being attentive to what God is already doing in their lives, and in the world, then it is within the worshiping community that this can best be done.

It is in worship, steeped in a Trinitarian Incarnational view of who God is and what God does, that the pastor can be most hopeful of leading the people of God in ways that are life changing and true to the Gospel. The pastor's work is not to lead the people, per se, but rather to lead them to God. It is as the people of God become part of the life of the Trinity that they find the necessary relationship for being the redeeming people of God in the world.

A New View of Pastoral Ministry

Staying centered, on course, being honest to the call, is such hard work. The central work of being a pastor is the work that no one sees, that which is done behind the scenes. Peterson,

The Pastor

in his book <u>Working the Angles</u> sets out the foundational work of the pastor as prayer, reading scripture, and giving spiritual direction. The pastor who seeks to point to the reality of God-with-us, as revealed in the Trinity, must first find this Trinitarian reality in their own lives. To be a faithful pastor is not to know the latest trends in contemporary worship or church growth principles. The pastor must first be one who knows a relationship with God that is transforming at the deepest levels of the soul. The most important work a pastor does in the parish is done before the sun rises, in the struggles of becoming a person, fully alive in Christ.

The work of the pastor which will most profoundly affect the life of the church can go almost unnoticed by the congregation. The work of the pastor that is most essential to being true to the call of ministry is work that in all probability will not be valued by the congregation but might even cause resentment because of the time it takes away from the more conspicuous acts of pastoring.

Eugene Peterson sees pastors being pressed into service not as pastors but as managers and shopkeepers.[1] It is our natural inclination to want to please the people who pay our salary. The easy road is to do the things that will get immediate attention and be rewarded with praise. To counter this pressure a pastor needs a vision of a God who is not removed but very

---

[1] Peterson tells an incredible story of how the committee that over saw him during the first years of his new church development handled their assignment. It seems he was required to make a regular report to them. The first page was a typical statistical report; the next couple of pages were to be a personal report of how the ministry was going. After realizing no one read past the first page he began writing a fictional report including drinking problems, sexual adventures, and the use of peyote in the Eucharist. The day he confronted them on their lack of support was a moment of humor but great disappointment for this minister. The denominational leaders cared little about anything beyond how well the church was doing numerically and how they were proceeding toward financial independence. Eugene H. Peterson, <u>Under the Unpredictable Plant</u> (Grand Rapids, Michigan: William B. Eerdmans Publishing Company, 1992), 78-80.

active in our ministries. A Trinitarian Incarnational view of God gives us the vision we need for doing ministry. The success of our ministries is not a result of what we do, but rather, as in worship, our entering into what God is already doing. So the pastor needs to start her/his day, not list-making for what she/he will do today, but being attentive to God and what God is doing in God's work of redeeming the world. This attentiveness allows the pastor to enter into what God is already doing. This attentiveness also gives the pastor insight into what God is doing in others' lives.

The Church, at its best, has understood the Trinity as a model for understanding the nature of God and God's work in the world through Jesus and the Holy Spirit. The doctrine of the Trinity is the means by which the church describes God's very active involvement in the world and becomes the way we can see our invitation into this divine work.

The vision of a Trinitarian God has a wonderful effect on the life of ministry for me. I have found, like many others, the idea of the Trinity an effective icon in allowing me to see the nature of my work as pastor and Christian. As Roublev's icon draws me into a relationship with God that lacks hierarchal supremacy, so an appropriate understanding of the Trinity will allow us to understanding our work as part of a much greater ministry that God has already put into motion. The early church was taken up into a relationship with God which was solidly Trinitarian in practice. It is as we enter into the wisdom of those who have gone before us in the journey of becoming pastors that we can best serve God in the Church of Jesus Christ.

The place of preaching

As I approached God in a new way, as my understanding of how we relate to God changed by the influence of the doctrine of the Trinity, I found my understanding of the role of preaching had to change dramatically.

No longer did Sunday morning worship center on what I had to say and how I said it. Informed by a Trinitarian Incarnational view of worship the sermon became a sacrament of sorts. The sermon is just one more medium that God uses to bring people into a relationship with God's self. Preaching is not a place to expound on the preacher's great ideas of how to live.

The Pastor

When the preacher steps into the pulpit she/he does not speak for herself/himself but rather it is Christ who has taken center stage. We enter into something that God has already been doing. God has declared God's love for us in great acts of redemption, in daring steps of love, in words of justice and mercy. The preaching event is a supernatural act of God using a human being to share the love of Christ by the power of the Holy Spirit.[2] In Trinitarian Incarnational worship God takes center stage and the pastor/preacher becomes an agent used by God to God's glorious ends.

The pastor's role in transforming People
A Trinitarian understanding of God and a ministry that reflects this perspective also changed how I understood the role of the sovereignty of God in the lives of God's people. I had found I did a lot of protecting of God as though God could not take care of God's self. As in preaching, it seemed that if I did not make it happen, or I did not take the initiative, it would not get done. It was almost like God was only a bit player in worship and ministry and I was the one who had to be depended on to take care of things.

A Trinitarian Incarnational view of worship and ministry changes all of this. Through's God gracious acts, revealed in the Trinity, I find that I don't have to make it all happen, God has things in control. My job is to enter into what God is doing. This radically changes how I go about my job as pastor.

I do not have to protect God, I just need to be faithful in bringing people to the place where they can find an honest relationship with God for themselves. The beauty of God's Trinitarian relationship with God's people is that it is through relationship, and not by argument, that lives are changed and

---

[2] Victor Pentz in his Dr. of Ministry dissertation on Preaching speaks of an understanding of preaching where the event is seen as a supernatural act by God. Without using the word Trinity Pentz still speaks of the role of pastors/preachers as entering into what God is already doing. I would call it entering into the life of God's Trinitarian nature as revealed by God. Victor D. Pentz, <u>Preaching to Effect Transformation</u> (D.Min. diss. Fuller Theological Seminary, 1991).

transformed for God's glory in the world.

The pastor's primary work is not to articulate a political position or lead a march on city hall (though this could very well be a pastor's personal response to entering into God's work as he/she sees it).

This style of bringing people to God requires a trust in God's sovereignty. It also means trusting that God can work in others' lives as God has worked in yours. It is to believe that you are not necessarily in possession of the definitive word of God. It means that you have to trust that others, even those who hold different views from your own, are possibly inspired by the Holy Spirit in understanding the mind and will of God. It is scary work to trust that God really is sovereign and can take care of the work of salvation in the world.

The Sacraments

If the goal of the pastor's work is to bring folks near to God, that they might experience a Trinitarian relationship with God, then the pastor's greatest tools are the churches' sacraments.

When a church allows baptism to become a "cute" family ceremony relegated to the early service, it misses the vitality of the act of baptism to define and empower the Christian church. It is only through the waters of baptism that the church can be the church. It should be made clear to every member of the congregation, each time the sacrament is enacted, that this is the defining moment in the life of the church. It is not what we do that makes the church but what God is doing in us. In infant baptism, particularly, we recognize it is not what we do that makes us worthy of being in God's family but it is purely an act of God's grace. It is in the waters of baptism that we are made one in Christ's baptism. It is in the waters of baptism that we are initiated into the family of God on earth and in heaven. It is through the waters of baptism that we find the spirit to be the people of God.

Baptism reminds us of who we are and what we should be about as God's people.

Baptism should play a regular part in the worship experience of the church even when there are no baptisms to be celebrated. In the church I serve we have taken to celebrating a

The Pastor

service of re-affirmation of baptism twice a year as a congregation. This is a service where the liturgy and the sermon reflect on the meaning of our baptisms. The culmination of the service is an invitation for folks to come forward to the baptismal font to "remember your baptism and be thankful." The stress is on the reformed understanding that baptism is not an act of our goodness in coming to God but God's grace in calling us and making it possible for us to come at all.

We also celebrate a re-affirmation of baptism at important transitions in the life of our members. When we ordain and install new board members we remember God's promise and our response remembering and affirming our baptismal vows.

When we make baptism central to our understanding of life in Christ, we better understand the nature of living a Trinitarian life in God. Even our younger children are made aware of the rewards and obligations of baptism. We remind them graphically that they, as part of a baptized community, play an important role in guiding and nurturing the newly baptized. We remind them that their actions and words are a model that can play an important role in influencing the youngest members of the congregation in being Christ like.

Though the monthly celebration of the Lord's Supper has become normative in the church in recent years I believe anything short of a weekly celebration of the Lord's Supper by the whole congregation fails to be faithful to the scriptural witness, reformed theology, tradition, or good sense.

Calvin understood the need of a frequent celebration of the Lord's Supper for his congregation. Calvin wanted a weekly celebration of communion in Geneva. But weekly communion was not to be realized by Calvin.

The problem seemed to be that the people in his church were not accustomed to receiving the Lord's Supper on a regular basis. Though communion was performed often in the Roman Church of Calvin's day it was only received by the Priest most of the time. The meaning of the Eucharist was primarily of reenacting Christ's sacrifice. The service seemed to have become so holy and mystical that for people to participate was always a danger. The people in the pew were satisfied, and many even relieved, to just watch the priest during the Eucharistic service.

Putting the Trinity Back in the Church

Being in the same building as the priest during the breaking of the bread and the inaudible prayers of the holy meal had become the norm in the church.

In Calvin's day most of the people in the Roman Church only received the bread and the cup once a year on Easter. The emphasis was placed on great preparation of body and soul in making one ready for the reception of this holy meal on this very special day. With all this "preparation" and "getting ready" to receive the Lord's Supper Calvin, along with other reformers, sought to change the understanding of the Lord's Supper from an event to be watched to one of participation.[3] He still wanted a weekly celebration of the holy meal but he knew it should be one in which the people, and not just the priest, participated. The presence of Christ in the meal was still stressed by Calvin but not in the sense of flesh and blood but in a mystical union with the people in the celebration.

Calvin still laid a great deal of stress on people's being prepared to receive the elements. The service of communion was separated from and placed after the preaching part of the service, allowing those who had not been baptized or having yet received proper instruction in the faith to leave before the celebration. But the premise was that communion was to be a celebration of all the people and that active participation in the service in receiving the elements was necessary for perseverance in the Christian faith. The service was not just participation in the sacrifice of Christ but a participation in the community of all the saints.[4]

---

[3] Evidently the faithful who had been accustomed under the old order to receive communion but once a year just could not make that kind of transition, and so, quarterly observance became the rule.... A particularly good example of this was the way the Reformers wanted to restore to the church the weekly communion of the faithful. In Strasbourg Bucer and his colleagues tried to get the whole population of the city to come to one celebration of the Lord's Supper at the cathedral each Lord's Day. Unfortunately the Reformed pastors of Strasbourg were never able to bring about that reform. Old, 159.

[4] "...as the bread which is hallowed for the common use of us all is made from many grains so intermingled that it is impossible to

The Pastor

I see the wisdom of Calvin as we serve the people of God in our church in our day. How can we not see the rewards of being a people who not only hear the word of God preached each Sunday but participating in the Eucharist. When I have tried to introduce more frequent communion to the church I serve, the reaction by many is that it is too catholic or will become too ordinary or we just do not have time to include it in the service.

The truth is that the idea of weekly participation of all God's people in the service of communion was first the idea of the reformed church. It was not until very recently that the Catholic Church has tried to include all the people of God weekly in receiving the elements of the Eucharist. And how in the world could the Lord's Supper become ordinary? Surely, celebrating communion weekly might take away a personal high that comes with a quarterly or monthly participation in the meal. But this would surely be made up for in the rhythm of weekly participation of celebrating God's holy meal given to us as a gift for our faith.

What a weekly celebration of communion offers to the church is a visual and experiential understanding of God's ways with us. Is not God's invitation of faith to us an invitation to participate in and with God in wonderful acts of redemption for world and people? To come to the table weekly is to experience that we are not recruited by God to do God's work and then sent off to get the work done on our own. At the table we come to be in the family of the Trinity that has embraced us and allows us to live lives in and for and with Christ.

Just as my denomination (Presbyterian Church U.S.A.) makes it a requirement in its book of worship to never celebrate the Lord's Supper without the preaching of the word so it should, in my opinion, use strong language in encouraging the celebration of the Lord's Supper in response to every event of

---

distinguish them from one another. So ought we to be so united among ourselves in an indissoluble friendship. And what is more, we receive there one and the same Body of Christ so as to be made members of it." John Calvin. (This quote comes from the cover of a bulletin cover that had no reference.)

Putting the Trinity Back in the Church

preaching on the Lord's Day.

I am thankful for the wisdom of my denomination in opening the table to our baptized children. I believe it is in this act, of inviting our children to sit at table with us, that we witness the unmerited, transforming, healing grace of Christ working in us and for us and through us. Once our children are baptized they are really a part of the family to which God has called us. In inviting our children to the table we are acting out the belief that, in Jesus Christ, God really does call us to be part of the Family of God at the moment of our baptism. The only "understanding" I believe children need in coming to the table is to be part of a family that articulates and practices its faith and know how to drink from a cup.

Summary

It is a real loss for the church community to move away from making the sacraments of baptism and communion the central and defining acts of the life of the church. It is in these sacraments that we live out the life of God with us as expressed in the doctrine of the Trinity.

CHAPTER 10

THE PEOPLE

The promise of the Gospel is that we have not even begun to be the wonderful, productive, fulfilled, splendid people that we can expect. At the very heart of God's nature is a passion for restoring the creator's blessed image in each of God's created ones. The goal of Christian salvation is a people who love as God loves. God redeems humanity that their lives might be a blessing to all of creation.

The means for this holy transformation is not hidden nor esoteric in nature but rather clearly proclaimed and available to all.

THE GOOD NEWS REVEALED IN WORSHIP

The promise of the Gospel put us in a relationship with God that allows us to see ourselves for who we really are, fully human and fully alive. As we live out the life promised in God's revelation we enter into a life blessed by God's presence with us and in us and through us. We act now, not on our own, but in union with God. Our lives are transformed by the power of God-with-us made possible by God's open Trinitarian nature that draws us into the life of God.

The promise of the Gospel reveals a quality of "life-together" that we have only dreamed about in the past--a community which finds its roots in selflessness, truth, justice, and love, and where everyone is valued for her/his remarkable gifts. Our life-together becomes so intertwined with the life of the Trinity that it has the quality of reflecting this greater community.

My concern is that the church has missed the mark in presenting and sharing this Good News with its people.

We as a people are so inclined to revert back to our own self propeled means for salvation that the church needs to be clear and loud and explicit in presenting a Gospel that can not be corrupted by human means of grace.

I believe we, as a church, need to take the doctrine of the trinity seriously and see its composition as normative for relationships with God and each other. It is within the Doctrine of the Trinity that we can come to understand lives which are fruitful, fulfilling, and life giving. It is only in the context of knowing God in light of an active, open, alive, inviting, Trinity that we meet God as God really is. Our transformation into a people who can live up to God's high calling for us is only made possible by God's open invitation to life lived in Christ, by the power of the Holy Spirit, as an act of God's great love for all creation.

It is within a Trinitarian doctrine of God that we can witness the true nature of our life together. In our western culture, dominated by rugged individualists, the revelation of Trinitarian relationships defines the faithful as a counter culture dedicated to life lived in faithful and loving community.

This Christian counter culture is not asked to define nor sustain itself. The Christian community is not given a good idea and then thrown back on itself to find the resources to nourish itself and carry on.

As we understand the doctrine of the vicarious humanity of Christ we find a wonderful source of knowing how we can be successful in becoming the faithful people of God in word and deed. I find in Torrance's statement "He has become what we are that we might become what He is" a wealth of insight into the nature of being found in Christ in all areas of worship, life, and mission. It is not that we do it on our own but as we find ourselves "in Christ" we become faithful participants in the

The People

continuing acts of God.

When we come to worship we don't depend on our ability to worship rightly but we rest in Christ, and become part of the wonderfully full worship of Heaven. We can rightly be called a royal priesthood, a holy nation, God's own people, not because of anything we do or are but by the blessed gift of entering into the nature of Christ.

The church has been blessed with all the essentials needed for being a faithful, productive and authentically Christ like community, but we, particularly in the reformed church, have not availed ourselves to the fullest of what God has offered. Our worship has stressed the important place of the word preached at the expense of the word of God revealed in the breaking of the bread. In the mind of J.J. von Allmen we have ignored the most insightful minds of the church for 400 years by not recognizing the crucial role the sacraments play in Christian worship.

von Allmen sees the basic flaw in the reformed churches' pattern of worship as its lack of weekly celebration of the Lord's Supper. He concludes his work, <u>Worship: Its Theology and Practice</u>, with this observation about the fatal flaw of reformed worship "...because it (reformed worship) is blunted, without its edge, because it does not find its culmination and completion in the Eucharist..."[1] He believes that the church's worship cannot be all that it should be, a reflection and practice of the joyful and transforming worship of heaven, until we re-introduce the weekly communion service.

It is in the worshiping community that we come to know ourselves as we truly are. It is at the Lord's Table that we taste the first fruits of whom we were made to be. James Torrance states "...perhaps we are never more truly human than at the Lord's Table, where Christ draws us into his life of communion with the Father and into communion with one another."[2]

We are a community gathered together by God, shaped by a quality of life revealed as Trinitarian in nature. We are a

---

[1] von Allen, 312.

[2] Heron, 15, 16.

people clothed in Christ and renewed by the gift of the Holy Spirit. Our actions are now defined by baptism, being chosen by God, and maintained and nourished by participation in Holy Communion.

The only reason Christians of the early church had for committing their lives to the God of Abraham was the possibility of entering into the life of God as revealed in God's Trinitarian self revelation in history. It was to this dynamic relationship, with all its possibilies for giving meaning and substance to life that was at the heart beat of the early church.

It is in worship that we come to know, in theologically sound and impassioned ways, the presence of God in our lives. "The work of worship, then, is to bring people into a place that allows them to experience the fullness of the love of God revealed in all its glory through the work of Father, Son, and Spirit."[3]

SUMMARY

There is much to share with the people of God. The life of faith demands that every part of our life be touched and transformed by a new life lived in God. But we must start our journey at the center.

As in the early church we too find our center in the worshiping community. It is at worship that we are instructed and reminded of that which is to be normative in our lives. It is at worship that we come to experience community as it is meant to be lived. It is the actions of worship that we are made open to God's presence in our lives as real and tangible. It is in worship that we are invited into the worship on earth as it is in heaven.

The concept and historical fact that God has revealed God's self to us as Trinity, and that God has invited us to participate in this nature through the ministry of Christ and the

---

[3] Karl Shadley, Unpublished paper, Torrance's class on worship, spring 1992, 16.

The People

power of the Holy Spirit must be the starting place of our life of faith. Presenting to the people anything less is to deny them the very gospel that has the ability to save their lives.

CONCLUSION

"And now, what does it matter? It matters more than anything else in the world."[1]

These are the prophetic words of C.S. Lewis in speaking about the Doctrine of the Trinity. I agree with Lewis and La Cugna and the many others who now see the Doctrine of the Trinity as essential to the life and health of the Church of Jesus Christ. The Church must understand that the doctrine of the Trinity is a doctrine that gives to us a clear and passionate understanding of God and ourselves. Lewis goes on to explain his reasoning for passionately embracing the Doctrine of the Trinity.

> The whole dance, or drama, or pattern of this three-Personal life is to be played out in each one of us: Or (putting it the other way around) each one of us has got to enter that pattern, take his place in that dance. There is no other way to the happiness for which we were made. Good

---

[1] C.S. Lewis, Mere Christianity (New York: Macmillan Publishing Co., Inc., 1943), 153.

things as well as bad, you know, are caught by a kind of infection. If you want to get warm you must stand near the fire: if you want to be wet you must get into the water. If you want joy, power, peace, eternal life, you must get close to, or even into, the thing that has them. They are not a sort of prize which God could, if He chose, just to hand out to anyone. They are a great fountain of energy and beauty spurting up at the very center of reality. If you are close to it, the spray will wet you: if you are not, you will remain dry. Once a man is united to God, how could he not live forever? Once a man is separated from God, what can he do but wither and die?[2]

For me and for the many who have taken up "Trinity talk"[3] we sense a need to reclaim this old doctrine for what we believe was its intended use. The doctrine of the Trinity is an essential doctrine for the church because it alone allows us to see the mighty acts of God, Father, Son and Holy Spirit, as an act of the whole of who God is. The church must be enlightened by the premises that lie at the root of Trinitarian thought that was revealed to the first disciples of Christ. Though the early churches' articulation of the Trinity was not yet systematized, it was an understanding and experience of God as revealed equally as Father, Son, and Holy Spirit that birthed, inspired, and sustained the early church and its mission to the world.

It was in worship that the church found its deepest experience and so its understanding of what it meant to be part of God's Trinitarian nature. It was in worship that the church regularized the language that was to become it's self expression of who it was in relationship to God, each other, and the whole of creation. As the shape of worship, particularly in the

---

[2] Ibid., 153.

[3] This is Peter's term for those who have joined in the work of redeeming the term Trinity for practice and theology work today.

Conclusion

formulations of baptism and Holy Communion, was developed and revealed in the church, an understanding of God as Trinity became a part of the language of the liturgy.

It is the contention of this writer that the only place that we can find this experience of life, as lived out by Christ, is in the worshiping life of the church. It is in worship, both public and private, that we enter into a powerful relationship with Christ that reveals to us the dynamic nature of living a life "in Christ."

It cannot be overstated that it is only when the church understands itself in the light of its worship experience that it can truly be a community shaped by God and God's will for it. It is out of this worship experience that the church can find integrity in calling itself the body of Christ.

My goal for worship at the church I serve[3] is that our styles and forms for worship would be a visual model, for the people who worship with us, of what it means to live in a community that is already experiencing the reality of God acting in us and through us and for us every moment of our lives.

I don't believe that we will make this happen through new programs or new organizational structures or new forms of worship. These resources can be a support in our work, but they cannot be our starting point nor our guide. It is only when we come to worship in Christ and enter into the divine worship that is already going on for us that we will be a church that worships according to the will and desire of God. It is in worship that we come into a relationship with God that can renew us in God's image, as we are made one with Christ and indwelled with the Holy Spirit. It is from this place of Christian, Trinitarian Incarnational worship that we then find the direction and motivation for the living out of the Christian life.

POSTLUDE

It was a total surprise to me that when I wrote a book it was about the Trinity.

In College I received my early introduction to the doctrine of the Trinity. The lesson is still a vivid one to me. It was that old "God as three states (liquid, gas, solid) but still one". This anemic, non-relational, illustration left me cold and I never though much about the doctrine of the Trinity for many, many years. I never preached or taught about the Trinity and it was never a part of my thoughts in trying to understand my relationship with God. The idea of the Trinity for me was tied up with an esoteric understanding of God-up-there and a way of defending the worship of the One God while including the Spirit and Jesus in the mix.

This all changed in a two week Doctorate of Ministry class I had with Dr. James Torrance in 1990. It was James who baptized my imagination to a lively understanding of the Trinitarian nature of God involved in our world and in our lives, in my life. It as like a light went on that explained so much of my experience. I began to look with different eyes on Scripture and the books that has been such an important part of my faith development.

For James the Trinity was not some esoteric exercise but

a way of understand our relation with God as revealed by God. His understanding of the Trinity was not tied up in God-up-there but was the very nature of God as reconciler. His experience of the Trinity took him to Ireland and South Africa to share the good news that God is the living and active God of relationship and love.

This book has been a long time in the making. I began working on it in 1991 as part of the dissertation requirement for the Doctor of Ministry program at Fuller Theological Seminary. Much of the research for the book was done during a Sabbatical while I was on staff at Village Presbyterian Church in Arcadia California.

During this time of writing I had the gift of working with my friend Margaret Kolberg on the project. Margaret is gifted at "office practice" and made-up for my many shortcomings in this area. She typed and categorized on the computer thousands of quotes found in the books I was reading and proofed drafts of the dissertation. She also did many odd jobs like mailing books I needed to my mountain hideaway and even intervened with the bank for me during a checking boondoggle, all the while encouraging me when I thought maybe I wasn't up to this writing task.

When the opportunity for a Sabbatical was made available by my present Church (Calvary Presbyterian of Berkeley) I decided it was time to make my goal of putting my dissertation into a more readable book form was due. Most of the editing and rewriting was done at San Francisco Theological Seminary and completed on a retreat with my wife Myrna at a little cabin at our beloved Sea Ranch on the Northern California Coast.

I don't think a day goes by that my life in Christ is not informed and inspired by this lively and life giving doctrine of the Trinity. Praise be to God.

BIBLIOGRAPHY

Anderson, Ray S. God So Loved: A Theology for Ministry Formation. Huntington Beach, California: By the author, 4015 Humboldt Drive, 1995.

_____. ed. Theological Foundations for Ministry. Edinburgh: T. & T. Clark, Ltd. 1979.

Bajema, Edith. Worship: Not for Adults Only. Grand Rapids, Michigan: CRC Publications. 1990.

Barth, Karl. Church Dogmatics. Edited by G.W. Bromiley, T.F. Torrance. Translated by G.W. Bromiley. Edinburgh: T.&T. Clark. 1936, 1975. Vol.1, Part 1.

Bellah, Robert. Habits of the Heart: Individualism and Commitment in American Life. New York: Harper and Row Publishers. 1985.

Berryman, Jerome W. Godly Play: A way of religious education. San Francisco: Harper Collins Publishers. 1991.

Best, Harold M. Music Through the Eyes of Faith. San Francisco:

Putting the Trinity Back in the Church Harper Collins Publishers. 1993.

The British Council of Churches. The Forgotten Trinity: 1 A Selection of Papers presented to the BCC Stury Commission on the Trinitarian Doctrine Today. London: BBC/CCBI Inter-Church House. 1988.

_____. The Forgotten Trinity: 2 A Selection of Papers presented to the BCC Stury Commission on the Trinitarian Doctrine Today. London: BBC/CCBI Inter-Church House. 1989.

_____. The Forgotten Trinity: 3 A Selection of Papers presented to the BCC Stury Commission on the Trinitarian Doctrine Today. London: BBC/CCBI Inter-Church House. 1989.

Boff, Leonardo. Trinity and Society. translated by Paul Burns. New York: Orbis Books. 1986.

Book of Common Worship. Louisville, Kentucky: Westminster/John Knox Press. 1993.

Brown, Paul B. In and For the World: Bringing the Contemporary Into Christian Worship. Minneapolis: Fortress Press. 1992.

Brueggemann, Walter. Finally Comes the Poet: Daring Speech for Proclamation. Minneapolis: Fortress Press. 1998.

Calvin, John. Calvin: Theological Treatises. translated by J.K.S. Reid. Philadelphia: The Westminster Press.

Calvin, John. The Institutes of Christian Faith. Edited by John T. McNeill. translated by Ford Lewis Battles. Philadelphia: The Westminster Press. 1560.

Calvin, John. The Epistle of Paul The Apostle to the Hebrews and the First and Second Epistles of St. Peter. Calvin's Commentaries Series. Translated by William B. Johnston.

Biography

Grand Rapids, Michigan: Wm. B. Eerdmans Publishing Company. 1963.

Constitution of the Presbyterian Church (USA), Part 1, The Book of Confession. Louisville, Kentucky: The Office of the General Assembly. 1991.

Corbon, Jean. The Wellspring of Worship. translated by Matthew J. O'Connell. New York/Mahwah: The Paulist Press. 1980.

Danielou, Jean. God's Life in Us. Denville, New Jersey: Dimensions Books. 1969.

Fatula, Mary Ann, O.P. The Triune God of Christian Faith. Collegeville, Minnesota: A Michael Glazier Book, The Liturgical Press. 1990.

Forrester, Duncan, James I.H. McDonald and Gian Tellini. Encounter with God. Edinburgh: T.&T. Clark Limited. 1983.

Foster, Richard, J. Celebration of Discipline. New York: Harper and Row, Publishers. 1978.

George, Timothy. Theology of the Reformers. Nashville, Tennessee: Broadman Press. 1988.

Gunton, Colin. Enlightenment and Alienation: An Essay towards a Trinitarian Theology. Grand Rapids, Michigan: William B. Eerdmans Publishing Company. 1985.

Hoon, Paul Waitman. The Integrity of Worship. Nashville: Abingdon Press. 1971.

Jasper, Ronald C.D. ed. Worship and the Child. London: The Joint Liturgical Group, SPCK. 1975.

_____. ed. The Renewal of Worship: essays by members of th Joint Liturgical Group. London: Oxford University Press. 1965.

Keifert, Patrick R. Welcoming the Stranger. Minneapolis: Fortress Press. 1992.

Kelly, Anthony, CSSR. The Trinity of Love; A Theology of the Christian God. New Theology Series, Gen. Ed. Peter C. Phan, Wilmington, Delaware: Michael Glazier. 1989.

Kettler, Christian, D. and Todd H. Speidell. Edit. Incarnational Ministry: The Presence of Christ in Church, Society, and Family (Essays in Honor of Ray S. Anderson). Colorado Springs, Colorado: Helmers & Howard. 1990.

LaCugna, Catherine Mowry. ed. God in Communion With Us: The Trinity. chap. in Freeing Theology: The essentials of theology in feminist perspective. New York, NY: Harper Collins Publishers Inc. 1993.

_____. God For Us: The Trinity and Christian Life. San Francisco: Harper. 1973.

Liesch, Barry. People in the Presence of God. Grand Rapids, MI: Zondervan Publishing House. 1988.

Leith, John, H. Basic Christian Doctrine. Louisville, Kentucky: Westminster/John Knox Press. 1993.

Lewis, C.S. Mere Christianity. New York, N.Y.: Macmillan. 1943.

Martin, Ralph P. The Worship of God: Some Theological, Pastoral, and Practical Reflections. Grand Rapids, Michigan: William B. Eerdmans Publishing Company. 1982.

Meeks, Douglas. Theology Today: review of "The Trinity and the Kingdom of God" by J. Moltmann. 38:472-477. Jan. 1982.

McKim, Donald K. Ed. Encyclopedia of the Reformed Faith. Louisville, Kentucky: Westminster/John Knox Press. 1992.

_____. Ed. Major Themes in the Reformed Tradition. Grand

Rapids, Michigan: William B. Eerdmans Publishing Company. 1992.

Moultmann, Jurgen. History and the Triune God: Contributions to Trinitarian Theology. New York, NY. Crossroads. 1992.

_____. The Trinity and the Kingdom: The Doctrine of God. Translated by Margaret Kohl. San Francisco: Harper & Row, Publishers. 1981.

Moltmann-Wendel, Elisabeth and Jurgen Moltmann. Humanity in God. Cleveland, Ohio: The Pilgrim Press. 1983.

Ng, David and Virginia Thomas. Children in the Worshiping Community. Atlanta, Georgia: John Knox Press. 1981.

Nouwen, Henri, J.M. Behold the Beauty of the Lord: Praying with Icons. Notre Dame, Indiana. Ave Maria Press. 1987.

_____. The Wounded Healer. New York, London, Toronto, Sydney, Auckland: An Image Book, Doubleday. 1979.

Oden, Thomas C. Pastoral Theology: Essentials of Ministry. San Francisco: Harper & Row, Publishers. 1983.

_____. The Transforming Power of Grace. Nashville: Abingdon Press. 1993.

O'Donnell, John, J. The Mystery of the Triune God. New York: Paulist Press. 1989.

Old, Hughes Oliphant. Guides to the Reformed Tradition: Worship. Atlanta: John Knox Press. 1984.

_____. Themes and Variations for a Christian Doxology: Some Thoughts on the Theology of Worship. Grand Rapids, Michigan: William B. Eerdmans Publishing Company. 1992.

_____. The Shaping of the Reformed Baptismal Rite in the Sixteenth Century. Grand Rapids, Michigan: William B.

Eerdmans Publishing Company. 1992.

Otto, Rudolf. The Idea of the Holy. translated by John W. Harvey. London: Oxford University Press. 1924.

Pentz, Victor, D. Preaching to Effect Transformation. D.Min. Dissertation Fuller Theological Seminary, 1991.

Peterson, David. Engaging with God: A Biblical Theology of Worship. Grand Rapids, Michigan: William B. Eerdmans Publishing Company. 1992.

Peterson, Eugene H. Answering God: The Psalms as Tools for Prayer. San Francisco: Harper & Row, Publishers. 1989.

_____. The Contemplative Pastor, returning to the art of spiritual direction. Dallas, Texas: Word Publishing. 1989.

_____. Under the Unpredictable Plant: An Exploration in Vocational Holiness. Grand Rapids, Michigan: William B. Eerdmans Publishing Company. 1992.

_____. Working the Angles: The Shape of Pastoral Integrity. Grand Rapids, Michigan: Williams B. Eerdmans Publishing Company. 1987.

Peters, Ted. God as Trinity: Relationality and the Temporality in Divine Life. Louisville, Kentucky: Westminster/John Knox Press. 1993.

_____. God the Trinity. chap. in God - the world's Future: Systematic Theology for a Postmodern Era. Minneapolis: Fortress Press. 1992.

Rahner, Karl. The Trinity. Translated by Joseph Donceel. New York: Herder and Herder. 1970.

_____. Foundations of Christian Faith: An introduction to the idea of Christianity. New York, NY: The Crossroad

Publishing Company. 1993.

Rice, Howard L. Reformed Spirituality: an introduction for believers. Louisville, Kentucky: Westminster/John Knox Press. 1991.

Richardson, Alan. ed. A Dictionary of Christian Theology. Philadelphia: The Westminster Press. 1969. S.v. "Theology of Mission," by R.M.C. Jeffery.

Richardson, Cyril, The Doctrine of the Trinity. New York: Abingdon, 1958.

Saliers, Don, E. Worship as Theology: Foretaste of Glory Divine. Nashville: Abingdon Press. 1994.

Sayers, Dorothy L. The Whimsical Christian, 18 Essays. New York, NY: Collier Books, Macmillan Publishing Company. 1987.

Schmemann, Alexander. For the Life of the World. : St. Vladimir's Seminary Press. 1973.

Smail, Thomas A. Reflected Glory. Grand Rapids, Michigan: William B. Eerdmans Publishing Company. 1975.

Smedes, Lewis B. Union with Christ. Grand Rapids, Michigan: William B. Eerdmans Publishing Company. 1970.

Stewart, Sonja M., and Jerome W. Berryman. Young Children and Worship. Louisville, Kentucky: Westminster/John Knox Press. 1998.

Torrance, James B. "The Place of Jesus Christ in Worship" in Theological Foundations for Ministry. ed. by Ray S. Anderson. Grand Rapids, Michigan: Eerdmans Publishing. 1979.

Torrance, T.F. The Mediation of Christ. Colorado Springs: Helmers and Howard. 1992.

_____. Trinitarian Perspectives: Toward Doctrinal Agreement. Edinburgh: T&T Clark. 1994.

Underhill, Evelyn. Worship. New York, NY: Crossroad. 1936.

von Balthasar, Hans Urs. Prayer. trans. Graham Harrison, San Francisco: Ignatius Press. 1955.

Wainwright, Geoffrey. Doxology: The Praise of God in Worship, Doctrine, and Life (A Systematic Theology). New York, NY. Oxford University, Press. 1980.

Wainwright, Arthur, W. The Trinity and the New Testament. London: S.P.C.K. 1962.

Webber, Robert E. Celebrating Our Faith: Evangelism Through Worship. San Francisco: Harper and Row Publishers. 1986.

_____. Worship is a Verb. Dallas, Texas: Word Publishing. 1985.

_____. Worship Old and New. Grand Rapids, Michigan: The Zandervan Corporation. 1982.

White, James F. Protestant Worship: Traditions in Transition. Louisville, Kentucky: Westminster/John Knox Press. 1989.

Willmon, William H. The service of God: Christian Work and Worship. Nashville: Abingdon Press. 1983.

_____. and Robert L. Wilson. Preaching and Worship in theSmall Church. Creative Leadership Series ed. by Lyle Schaller. Nashville: Abingdon Press. 1980.

_____. & Stanley Hauerwas. Preaching to Strangers. Louisville, Kentucky: Westminster/John Knox Press. 1992.

_____. Peculiar Speech: Preaching to the Baptized. Grand Rapids, Michigan: William B. Eerdmans Publishing

Biography

Company. 1992.

_____. Worship as Pastoral Care. Nashville: Abingdon Press. 1979.

_____. Word, Water, Wine and Bread, how worship has changed over the years. Valley Forge: Judson Press. 1980.

www.ingramcontent.com/pod-product-compliance
Lightning Source LLC
Chambersburg PA
CBHW030417100426
42812CB00028B/2993/J